# TANROKUBON

Foreword and Synopses by Ryūshin Matsumoto
Translated and Adapted by Mark A. Harbison

# TANROKUBON

## Rare Books of
## Seventeenth-Century Japan

Kogorō Yoshida

KODANSHA INTERNATIONAL LTD.
Tokyo, New York and San Francisco

With the exception of the names on the title page, all Japanese names in this book are given in Japanese style, with the surname first.

Distributed in the United States by Kodansha International/USA Ltd., through Harper & Row, Publishers, 10 East 53rd Street, New York, New York 10022.

Published by Kodansha International Ltd., 12–21 Otowa 2-chome, Bunkyo-ku, Tokyo 112 and Kodansha International/USA Ltd., with offices at 10 East 53rd Street, New York, New York 10022 and at The Hearst Building, 5 Third Street, Suite 430, San Francisco, California 94103. Printed in Japan.

*First edition, 1984*

**Library of Congress Cataloging in Publication Data**

Yoshida, Kogorō, 1902–83
   Tanrokubon, rare books of seventeenth-century Japan.
   Includes index.
   1. Printing—Japan—History—17th century. 2. Illustrated books—17th century—Catalogs. 3. Rare books—Japan—Catalogs. 4. Illustration of books—17th century—Japan. 5. Popular literature—Japan—Publishing. 6. Japanese literature—17th century—Publishing. 7. Books and reading—Japan—History—17th century. I. Matsumoto, Ryūshin, 1926–   . II. Harbison, Mark A. III. Title. IV. Title: Tanrokubon, rare books of 17th century Japan. V. Title: Rare books of seventeenth-century Japan.
Z186.J3Y68 1984     686.2'0952     83-48289
ISBN 4-7700-1134-2
ISBN 0-87011-634-7 (Kodansha International/USA)

# Contents

Foreword   6

Preface   8

1. The Development of *Tanrokubon* and the Period of Their Publication   11
   The Tradition of Hand-colored Illustrations   11
   *Nara-ehon*: Hand-written Texts and Hand-colored Illustrations   12
   Printed Books with Illustrations: The *Sagabon* Editions   14
   The Murky Origins and Rapid Decline of *Tanrokubon*   16

2. The Art of *Tanrokubon* Illustrations                              17
   The Dimensions and Composition of *Tanrokubon* Editions   17
   The Townsman Painters and Their Traditional Styles   19
   Colors: Considering the Cost   21

3. *Tanrokubon* as Literature                                        24
   *Tanrokubon* Editions in the Context of Publishing   24
   Classification by Literary Genre   26

4. The Term *Tanrokubon*                                             32
   Oldest References to a Modern Coinage   32
   A Term of the Taishō Era   34

*Tanrokubon* Illustrations and Synopses of the Texts                 37
   A Classical Tale (*Ko-monogatari*)   37
   War Tales (*Gunki Monogatari*)   41
   *Kōwakamai* Librettos (*Kōwaka Bukyoku*)   75
   *Otogizōshi*   121
   *Kanazōshi*   177
   Old *Jōruri* Librettos (*Ko-jōruri Shōhon*)   191

Illustrated Catalogue of Extant *Tanrokubon* Editions               199

Notes   211

Glossary   215

Selected Bibliography   225

Index   227

# Foreword

A much earlier graduate of our alma mater, Keiō University, Yoshida Kogorō was always for me a respected friend and mentor. Hailing from Kashiwazaki in Niigata Prefecture, Yoshida-*sensei* received his degree from the Faculty of Letters in 1924 and immediately assumed a teaching position in the Keiō University Elementary School. He remained there for more than forty years, until his retirement in 1965. During the crucial period from 1947 to 1956, when Japanese educators were struggling desperately to rebuild the educational system after the destruction of the Second World War, he served as principal of the Keio University Elementary School, never failing in his passionate dedication to the education of Japanese young people, who would bear responsibility for the country's future.

Yoshida-*sensei* will be best remembered for his public role as one of Japan's leading educators, but he also left behind an impressive record as a scholar. After graduating with a degree in history, he continued to pursue his interest in Euro-Japanese relations, and he is particularly well known for his work in the history of Christianity in Japan. His representative work is *Nihon Kirishitan Shūmon-shi*, a translation of Leon Pages's *History of Japanese Christianity*. This work, which was first published by Iwanami Bunko in 1938, must have been an extraordinarily difficult undertaking in a period when there was no reliable source material to aid the scholar in determining foreign place names and personal names, and there were few scholars willing to exert so much effort for a translation of a foreign work on Japanese history. That he was so uncompromising in his pursuit of truth during such a period is an excellent reflection of Yoshida-*sensei*'s stature as a scholar, and the fact that this work is now in its eleventh printing is evidence of his standing in the scholarly community.

Yoshida-*sensei* also possessed a rich sensitivity to art. He was particularly gifted with a unique appreciation of pictures. In 1973, he published his *Nihon no Sekihan-ga* (Japanese Stone Prints), and of course the present volume is the result of more than forty years of collecting and studying *tanrokubon* editions, of which Yoshida-*sensei*'s collection is the largest in the world. No one else could have produced the present volume.

Published in the early seventeenth century, *tanrokubon* were printed books with woodblock illustrations colored individually by hand. Because the principal colors employed in illustrations were *tan* (orange-red) and *roku* (mineral green), these books have come to be called *tanrokubon* (orange-red mineral-green books), but it is probably more accurate to refer to them as *tanroku-eiribon* (books with *tanroku*-colored illustrations).

There is a long tradition of woodblock printing and illustration in Japan, particularly in books and scrolls produced by the Buddhist establishment. However, it was not until the Keichō era (1596–1615) that woodblock and movable wooden type printing techniques began to make their appearance in literature and other secular books. Finally, in the Genna (1615–24) and Kanei (1624–44) eras, there was a great flood of printed books with illustrations. These books contained the texts of popular genres of medieval literature, which previously had been read in hand-copied scrolls and books. Most of these books were *tanrokubon*, with hand-colored illustrations.

The popular genres of medieval literature had gained a wide audience by the Muromachi period (1392–1573), during which they were published in scrolls (*emakimono*) or *Nara-ehon*, a type of illustrated book produced entirely by hand. The literary texts of *tanrokubon* bear a close resemblance to these earlier types of books. Some scholars believe that the color illustrations in *tanrokubon* are a similar attempt to imitate the illustrations in *Nara-ehon*. While it is true that the painting styles employed are usually quite similar, there are important differences in techniques of coloring. The coloring of *Nara-ehon* illustrations displays great care and an attempt to achieve realistic color compositions. Moreover, all of the space in each illustration is colored. *Tanrokubon* illustrations employ only two to five colors, which are scattered over the woodblock-printed outlines at random. There is no attempt at realistic depiction of colors. One explanation for this is that the requirements of mass production made it impossible to achieve the techniques of *Nara-ehon* illustration. However, the method of hand-coloring employed in *tanrokubon* is unique, suggesting that there may be other reasons for this unusual synthesis. Yoshida-*sensei* points out, for example, that *tanrokubon* may have been influenced by incunabula and old maps from the West. This is an extremely interesting theory, and one that certainly demands further research.

*Tanrokubon* illustrations were colored by amateurs employing extremely simple techniques, but strangely enough they possess an irresistible charm, suggestive of the simple beauty of coloring techniques employed in folkcrafts. Yoshida-*sensei* felt more strongly drawn to these simple, even crude illustrations than to the more carefully hand-colored original paintings that illustrate *Nara-ehon*. It is in his love for these early Japanese woodblock prints that one discovers his unique artistic sensibility and his highly individual personality. Japanese woodblock prints have become famous due to the popularity of *ukiyo-e* prints, but Yoshida-*sensei* has discovered a much older beauty in the woodblock illustrations of *tanrokubon*. I believe that it is highly significant that his collection is being introduced to the world in this volume.

Tragically, Yoshida-*sensei* died last year at the age of eighty-one, only a few months before the publication of his book, which will introduce the beauty of his beloved *tanrokubon* not only to the Japanese, but to people all over the world.

Matsumoto Ryūshin

# Preface

I am by nature the type of person who gets excited about beautiful pictures and books. Certainly I was moved to excitement by my first encounter with *tanrokubon*. It must have been forty or fifty years ago that I was first shown a *tanrokubon* edition by my dear friend Yokoyama Shigeru. (Professor Yokoyama passed away on 8 October 1980, leaving behind a reputation as one of the foremost specialists in textual scholarship in medieval Japanese literature.)

In those days, if one went off to a bookstore or library in search of *tanrokubon* editions, one was met with an awkward silence or a bewildered stare. After several such misadventures, I resolved to seek again the advice of Professor Yokoyama. He advised me that well-established bookstores specializing in traditional Japanese books occasionally listed *tanrokubon* editions in their catalogues, and that a number of editions could be seen in the collections of the Tōyō Bunko and the Japanese literature departments of major universities.

At first, I resigned myself to looking at *tanrokubon* editions in these collections, but soon I began to feel that I really must have at least one edition of my own. This condition grew steadily worse, and finally my obsession with *tanrokubon* became so well known among booksellers that they began to let me know whenever an edition was available. Nevertheless, *tanrokubon* are extremely rare, and one is seldom able to obtain the edition one wants on request. Indeed, in the four or five decades since I began, I have finally just managed to collect forty or fifty *tanrokubon* editions.

I would like to avail myself of the opportunity provided by this preface to express my deep debt of gratitude to the many people who contributed to the publication of this book. My first and most heartfelt thanks must go to my dear friend Professor Matsumoto Ryūshin, who prepared summaries of all the stories that appear in my editions and spent long hours putting the collection in order. A second debt of gratitude is owed to Professor Yokoyama Shigeru, who inspired my early interest in *tanrokubon*, and his wife Yokoyama Ai, who has been kind enough to permit me to include five editions from her late husband's collection (*Hioke no Sōshi, Chikubujima no Honji, Bunshō Sōshi, Kodaibu,* and *Chūshō*). I would also like to give special thanks to Mark A. Harbison, himself a specialist in medieval Japanese literature, who translated and adapted the Japanese text and provided additional notes and bibliographical information concerning current scholarship in English on the literary genres of *tanrokubon*. In addition, Tawara Yūsaku and Yoshida Yoshihiko provided immeasurable support. Finally, the tireless efforts of Suzuki Takako, Takahashi (Hayakawa) Keiko, and Lisa Oyama of Kodansha International cannot go unmentioned.

Yoshida Kogorō

A scene from *Gikeiki* (The Chronicle of Yoshitsune) reproduced
on *washi* (Japanese paper).

# The Development of *Tanrokubon* and the Period of Their Publication

THE TRADITION OF HAND-COLORED ILLUSTRATIONS

In 1841, Ryūtei Tanehiko (1783–1842), a famous author and playwright who wrote in every conceivable genre of Edo popular literature, published a collection of miscellany entitled *Yōshabako* (My Box for Things to Use and Things to Dispose Of). Tanehiko included in this collection copies in his own hand of librettos for old *jōruri* (*ko-jōruri*) and *sekkyō-bushi* (see Glossary). In the preface to these texts, Tanehiko writes:

> The three editions I have copied here are crudely executed examples of old *edoribon* [*tanrokubon*]. Red, green, and indigo have been scattered randomly, as if the wielder of the brush had let it wander where it might over deeply etched woodblock-printed lines. They are exquisite in their classical elegance.[1]

Tanehiko has stated wonderfully the contradictory nature of *tanrokubon*—their apparent crude simplicity and their strangely bewitching literary and artistic effects. Products of the early Edo period (1603–1868),[2] *tanrokubon* united new techniques of woodblock printing with popular literary genres of the Muromachi period (1392–1573) in a unique synthesis that not only deserves our attention in its own right but also carried the seeds of much that was to follow in the explosion of popular culture during the Edo period.

*Tanrokubon* were part of a much larger phenomenon of the two and a half centuries of the Edo period, during which new techniques of woodblock printing sparked a rapid expansion of publishing activity and large numbers of books began to appear in which both the text and illustrations were produced by exploiting these new techniques. Among these new books, which are generally called "illustrated block-printed editions" (*e-iri kanpon*), there were a number in which colors were applied by hand to enhance monochrome block-printed illustrations. The Japanese names of two of these colors, orange-red (*tan*) and mineral green (*roku*), plus the word for book (*hon*), comprise the elements of the term *tanrokubon*, the designation for these early block-printed and hand-colored editions which has gained currency among art historians and collectors.

In fact the tradition of applying colors by hand to block-printed pictures or illustrated manuscripts began in the Muromachi period, long before the development of *tanrokubon*. As is true of the tradition of woodblock printing itself, the earliest examples of this synthesis of techniques are to be found in Buddhist prints (*bukkyō hanga*) and printed illustrated scrolls (woodblock *emakimono*). *Yūzū Nenbutsu Engi* (Ōei era, 1394–1428), perhaps the most famous example, was lost in the Great Kantō Earthquake of 1923. Other examples still extant include the *Jūni Ten-zō*, the *Shingon Hasso-zō*, and the *Ryōgai Mandara*. Later in the Muromachi period, Buddhist prints such as *Kōya Daishi Gyōjō Zuga* and printed scrolls in which various techniques of applying color by hand were employed became fairly common.[3]

### *NARA-EHON*: HAND-WRITTEN TEXTS AND HAND-COLORED ILLUSTRATIONS

Perhaps due to the wonderful artistic effects of calligraphy, Japan also has a long tradition of combining literary texts with pictorial art. From the Kamakura period (1185–1392), this synthesis was achieved principally in illustrated scrolls (*emakimono*) and *Nara-ehon*. Unlike *tanrokubon*, however, illustrated scrolls and *Nara-ehon* were produced by and for the aristocracy, which was comprised of the court nobility, the highest ranks of the ruling warrior class, and the elite of the medieval Buddhist establishment. The current view among art and literary historians is that *tanrokubon* developed as an attempt to imitate the hand-written *Nara-ehon* by exploiting newly imported techniques of woodblock printing. This view was first advanced by Mizutani Futō in his seminal study *Kanazōshi*:

> The oldest [Japanese books] in which both text and illustrations were produced by woodblock printing are the *Sagabon* texts of *Ise Monogatari* and *Jūnidan Sōshi*. Current scholarly opinion places the dates of their publications in the Keichō era (1596–1615). . . . It seems likely that the concept of illustrating woodblock-printed books was suggested by illustrated scrolls, and it is important to note that *Nara-ehon*, which may themselves be regarded as reduced, booklet versions of illustrated scrolls, were already being produced on a large scale.
>
> I have not yet studied the subject of *Nara-ehon* in depth, and therefore I am unqualified to advance a theory of their origin, or to suggest criteria for determining which texts should be classified as *Nara-ehon*. If the term is employed to encompass all old books with calligraphy and color illustrations, it should include the "large upright books" [*ōgatabon*, usually 28 cm in height, 18.5 cm in width] produced before the Keichō era. However, the books that are generally called *Nara-ehon* today are the "oblong books" [*yokohon*, 16 cm in height, 24 cm in width], which were produced much later.
>
> It seems likely that the origins of *tanrokubon* may be traced to attempts to apply the techniques of coloring employed in *Nara-ehon* to illustrations produced by woodblock printing.[4]

While Professor Mizutani's theory concerning the origins of *tanrokubon* has gained currency, it leaves us with the question of what, in fact, *Nara-ehon* are. As in the case of *tanrokubon*, the term *Nara-ehon* itself seems to have been coined during the Meiji era (1868–1912), and its definition is by no means clear.[5] Judging from the term alone, it would seem to refer to the books produced in large numbers between the late sixteenth and early eighteenth centuries in which *Nara-e* (Nara pictures) were employed as illustrations for texts copied by hand in the flowing, cursive style of calligraphy. However, such a definition immediately presents a number of difficulties, not the least of which is the term *Nara-e* itself.

One theory holds that *Nara-e* were produced by artists associated with the *e-dokoro* (painting bureau) of the Kasuga Shrine in Nara, while another suggests that the term derives from the fact that the priests of Nara (*Nara hōshi*) who were producing Buddhist paintings and prints also applied their skills to illustrations for *Nara-ehon* texts of classical and popular literature. According to the latter theory, these illustrations should be called *nanto-e* (southern capital paintings). In fact, such a distinction is meaningless. Since Nara was the "southern capital," *nanto-e* is merely another way of saying *Nara-e*.

At this stage in our research on *Nara-ehon*, it is virtually impossible to offer a theory of their origins that would be acceptable to everyone. A number of specialists argue that the terms themselves suggest at least that *Nara-e* and *Nara-ehon* must have originated in Nara, but this is not supported by any substantial evidence. Moreover, even if the first *Nara-ehon* were produced in Nara, it is difficult to believe that all, or even most of them, were. It seems more likely that a great number of them were produced in Kyoto and Sakai. In this regard, *Yokohama-e* (Yokohama pictures) provide a good cautionary example. These late *ukiyo-e* prints, which were popular in the last decades of the Edo period and the first of the Meiji era, were actually published more widely in Edo than in Yokohama.

In order to arrive at a workable definition of *Nara-ehon*, we will need to examine their physical format as well as their literary contents, which are similar to those of *tanrokubon*. Early *Nara-ehon*, those produced before and during the Keichō era, were illustrated scrolls in various sizes or "large upright books." However, most extant *Nara-ehon*, which number in the thousands, were produced during the mid-seventeenth and early eighteenth centuries, and of these the "oblong book" format is represented by far more examples.

These books are bound in a style called *kochōsō*, which was modeled on books imported from Ming China. The paper is one of two types. *Torinoko-gami* is a good quality paper of egg-shell hue with a hard, lustrous surface. *Maniai-gami* has similar characteristics but is of a lesser quality. The calligraphy is executed in gorgeous cursive styles employing both Chinese characters and the Japanese *kana* syllabary. Illustrations are usually in traditional Japanese painting styles (*Yamato-e*), but there are also *Nara-ehon* illustrations in the style of the Kanō school and other schools of Japanese and Chinese painting. The illustrations are polychrome, often employing rich, vivid pigments and occasionally gold or silver leaf.

Covers display a variety of styles. The most common are the *uchi-gumori* cover, which employs *torinoko-gami* decorated with cloud patterns, and the *konshi kingindei* cover, a deep blue cover with patterns of flowers and grasses executed in gold or silver leaf. One occasionally sees covers executed in gold brocade with title papers of vermilion, silver leaf, or gold leaf pasted on, but these gorgeous creations are rare.

As stated above, illustrations are usually in the *Yamato-e* style. However a wide variety of schools are represented, including the prestigious Kanō school, as well

as the Tosa school. There are a number of exquisite illustrations in the *Nara-ehon* of the Keichō era and earlier periods, though some people may find them rather artless. On the other hand, my own opinion is that there are few illustrations in the *Nara-ehon* of the Kanbun era (1661–73) or subsequent periods that invite serious appreciation. If *Nara-ehon* did in fact exert a significant influence on *tanrokubon* therefore, the influence must be traced to the illustrated scrolls and "large upright books" of the earlier period.

## PRINTED BOOKS WITH ILLUSTRATIONS: THE *SAGABON* EDITIONS

Here it is essential to reconsider the history of illustration in printed scrolls and books in Japan. Perhaps as far back as the Kamakura period, and certainly throughout the Muromachi period, the tradition was dominated almost exclusively by the institutions of the Buddhist establishment, which was heavily influenced by Chinese and Korean Buddhism. The most famous extant examples of printed manuscripts with illustrations from these periods are the *Bussei Biku Rokumotsu-zu*, printed in 1246 by the priest Dōkyū of Sennyū-ji in Kyoto; the Yuryōho edition of *Buppō Shōshūki*, printed in 1348; and the *Jūgyū-zu* illustrations in the Gozan Buddhist editions of Shiburoku and Gomizen. Later, from the beginning of the Edo period, there are such well-known printed texts as *Teikan Zusetsu* (1606) and *Kunshin Zuzō* (1610). These, however, are merely reproductions of Korean and Chinese texts produced by copying the original woodblocks.

The extant examples of printed texts with rudimentary illustrations produced in Japan during the early years of the Edo period may, however, be counted on one hand: *Kadensho* (late Keichō era, 1596–1615), a reproduction of Zeami's famous treatise on Nō; *Sendenshō* (late Keichō era), a treatise on flower arranging; *Shūkaishō* (late Keichō era), containing illustrations traditionally held to be reproductions of paintings by the eighth-century priest Gyōki; *Gokyō*, or the Go Sutra; and *Tōken Meiran*, a treatise on Japanese swords. As important examples of early woodblock prints, the illustrations in these books are extremely interesting, but they do not merit aesthetic appreciation.

The technology of copperplate movable type printing was imported from Korea during the Korean campaigns of Toyotomi Hideyoshi in 1592 and 1596, and new printing techniques employing movable wooden type (ironically, now called "old type printing" [*ko-katsuji*]) were soon developed on the Korean model. This new movable wooden type technology sparked a rapid expansion in publishing, which included the production of printed editions of Japanese literary texts, both in Chinese (*kanbun*) and Japanese.

The publication of the *Sagabon* (Saga books) editions of *Ise Monogatari* and *Nijūshi-kō* marks the development of the first true printed books with illustrations in the Japanese tradition. These books were printed by the wealthy Kyoto merchants Honami Kōetsu (1558–1637) and Suminokura Soan (1571–1632) and were called *Sagabon* because Soan lived in the Saga district of Kyoto. The *Sagabon* editions of *Ise Monogatari* were lavishly produced, and the beauty of the paper, the bindings, and the covers has led many art historians to call the books themselves *objets d'art*. (I prefer to view them as products of craftwork.)

Research by Kawase Kazuma has revealed that as many as nine separate movable wooden type editions, as well as a woodblock edition of the *Sagabon Ise Monogatari*, were printed during the three-year period from 1608 through 1610.[6] In view of this, it is difficult to accept the theory advanced by many scholars that the *Sagabon* editions were distributed only among aristocratic patrons and close acquaintances of Suminokura Soan. Rather, Kawase's research suggests the extent to which the new illustrated texts captured the attention of people in all classes during the early Edo period.

The *Sagabon* editions of *Ise Monogatari* are bound in sets of two volumes each. There are twenty-five full-page illustrations in the first volume and twenty-three in the second volume. The monochrome illustrations are clearly in the traditional *Yamato-e* style of Japanese painting. Compared, however, to the care and expense that were lavished on the gorgeous paper, covers, and bindings, the illustrations, as well as the engraving techniques for calligraphy, display a gentle, easygoing aspect that produces a quite different effect, suggesting rather a subtle harmony and a quiet, understated refinement.

During the Keichō era, the *Sagabon* editions of *Ise Monogatari* were followed by a number of other new printed editions with illustrations, including *Fushimi Tokiwa*, *Kachō Fūgetsu*, *Jōruri Gozen Jūnidan Sōshi*, and *Ōgi no Sōshi*. By the end of the Genna era (1615–24), and especially during the Kanei era (1624–44), illustrated printed editions were being published in enormous quantities. However, none of these illustrations incorporated color. Print technologies were still in their infancy at this time, and, with only a few exceptions, experiments with applying colors to illustrations by exploiting print techniques were not yet being attempted.[7] As stated above, however, there was already a long tradition of applying colors by hand to Buddhist prints. Given the close relationship between the Buddhist establishment and publishing activity, all that was needed for this concept to be exploited in printed book illustrations was some stimulus from within the literary and artistic context of the period. Considering the intimate relationship between the two genres, this stimulus may have come from *Nara-ehon* as Professor Mizutani suggests, but other possible sources of influence exist as well. For example, the flood of printed books with color illustrations that were being imported from China during the period certainly should not be ignored.[8] Professor Yokoyama Shigeru has presented the highly imaginative theory that the development of *tanrokubon* was stimulated by exposure to the West:

> The period from the Keichō through the Kanei eras witnessed a great vogue for Western culture, and it is impossible to say that incunabula and other early Western book forms did not influence publishing technology in Japan. Indeed, among the books and maps imported from the West during this period, there are a number of editions in which coloring and printing techniques are virtually identical to those seen in *tanrokubon*.[9]

In short, research on *tanrokubon* has not yet progressed to the level at which a definitive explanation of the various influences on them may be advanced. Two of the woodblock editions of the *Sagabon Ise Monogatari*, for example, are thought

to have been published in the Genna era (1615–24); they both contain illustrations colored by hand and employing orange-red and mineral green pigments.[10] I myself have not seen these editions, and so it is impossible to say whether they should be regarded as *tanrokubon*.

THE MURKY ORIGINS AND RAPID DECLINE OF *TANROKUBON*

The whole question of when the earliest *tanrokubon* were produced is complicated by the sort of problems I have alluded to above. I have not seen even one example of a genuine *tanrokubon* bearing a colophon dated before the Kanei era (1624–44). However, besides the experiments with hand-colored woodblock illustrations in the two *Sagabon* editions of *Ise Monogatari* just referred to, there is a *kawaraban* edition (a book printed by a technique in which the text and illustrations were carved on a clay block that was then baked or dried) of *Ōsaka Abe no Kassen-zu* bearing a colophon that reads, "Seventh day, fifth month, Keichō 20" (1615). The illustrations in this text are crudely colored with orange-red and mineral green. The existence of this edition suggests that experiments with the techniques of *tanrokubon* had begun as early as the Keichō era.

It is clear that the "old movable type editions" (*ko-katsujibon*) of *tanrokubon* were being produced in the Genna era, and that by the Kanei era woodblock editions (*seihanbon*) were being produced in large numbers as well. Thus, we can assume with a reasonable degree of assurance that the first true *tanrokubon* were produced at the end of the Genna era. In general, however, the period that is most closely associated with *tanrokubon*, and the period during which the largest numbers were produced, is the Kanei era. Indeed, the great majority of extant *tanrokubon* could be called "Kanei editions" (*Kanei hanpon*), and this would by no means be a misnomer. There are very few extant *tanrokubon* from subsequent periods, and, in fact, they had lost much of their popularity by the Shōhō (1644–48) and Keian (1648–52) eras. By the Meireki (1655–58) and Manji (1658–61) eras, production of *tanrokubon* had ceased entirely.

There is perhaps no simple explanation for the precipitous decline of *tanrokubon*. It seems likely, however, that the high cost of producing them, resulting from the considerable time and skill required, and the relatively low rate of return on the publisher's investment encouraged publishers to seek more profitable formats for popular printed books. More than forty years had passed since the first *tanrokubon* had been published, and early enthusiastic readers had lost interest. By the 1650s, perhaps, they were satisfied with monochrome illustrations and were becoming interested more in new literary genres and individual artists with distinctive styles than in the effects made possible by applying colors to illustrations.

*Tanrokubon* bearing clearly dated colophons are extremely rare. The largest number of datable editions are those containing texts of old *jōruri* librettos or *sekkyō-bushi*. Datable *kōwakamai* librettos, *otogizōshi*, and *kanazōshi* editions are rare treasures indeed. I have listed on page 199 all of the *tanrokubon* editions thought to be extant.[11]

# The Art of *Tanrokubon* Illustrations

THE DIMENSIONS AND COMPOSITION OF *TANROKUBON* EDITIONS

While the texts of a number of *tanrokubon* were printed with the techniques of movable wooden type printing (*ko-katsuji*), all *tanrokubon* illustrations are woodblock prints, and it is for their hand-colored woodblock illustrations that I have come to value *tanrokubon* so highly. Even in Japan, when we think of woodblock prints, we almost always think first of *ukiyo-e*. We forget the many outstanding prints produced in earlier periods. I have mentioned, for example, a few of the ineffably beautiful woodblock prints produced in the great tradition of Buddhist pictorial art. Even within the genre of *ukiyo-e* itself, we overlook such early styles as *tan-e* (orange-red prints) and *urushi-e* (lacquer prints) in our fascination with the more voluptuous beauty of the *nishiki-e* (brocade prints) of Utamaro or Hiroshige.

Woodblock prints are appreciated today as works of art, but it is more appropriate to deal with them as craftwork. This is not to imply, of course, that craftwork should be held in lower esteem than art. Unlike original paintings, in which the artist is free to achieve his images directly, the woodblock print is inextricably bound to its medium. The artist's image is transformed in the processes of carving and printing, and thus the artistic effect itself is indirect. The further back we go in the tradition of Japanese woodblock prints, the more it is true that woodblock prints are not reproductions of original paintings but, rather, are pictures that came into being for the first time through the medium of printing. They do not exist except as woodblock prints. It is precisely this quality of woodblock prints that produced their mysterious, subtle effects.

However, the technology of woodblock printing improved during the Edo period, and woodblock prints became more and more like reproductions of original paintings. In fact, woodblock prints gradually lost the quality of indirect expression that characterizes the styles of the early Edo period. The illustrated books of the early Edo period represent the highest achievement of woodblock printing, and in them one finds some of the most beautiful prints in the world. *Tanrokubon* illustrations, with their bold printed lines and brushed-on colors, are the most outstanding of these early masterpieces.

A description of the physical format of *tanrokubon* should begin with a general classification of their dimensions. They are usually classified into the following four sizes, within which particular literary genres may be representative:

**Large-size Upright Books** (*ōbon*): Because they are printed on Mino paper, these books are sometimes called *Mino-ban*. The dimensions of a sheet of Mino paper are usually 37 cm by 28 cm. In the style of binding called *fukuro toji*, which is the most common in Japanese books, each sheet of paper is folded in half to form one "leaf"(*chō*) of the book, which consists of two pages of text and illustration (as in this book). The normal dimensions of large-size upright books, therefore, are 28 cm in height and 18.5 cm in width. War tales (*gunki monogatari*) in this form are numerous. One occasionally sees large-size *tanrokubon* that are somewhat narrower than is normal for editions in this classification.

**Medium-size Upright Books** (*chūbon* or *hanshibon*): Books in this form are bound in the same way as large-size upright books but employ a type of paper called *hanshi*, which has dimensions of 34 cm by 24 cm. Thus, their dimensions are usually 24 cm in height and 17 cm in width. Medium-size editions of *kōwakamai* librettos are representative.

**Oblong Books** (*yokohon*): 15.6 cm in height and 23 cm in width. Old *jōruri* librettos and a special subcategory of *otogizōshi* editions are most common.

**Small-size Books** (*kohon* or *kogatabon*): 19.5 cm in height and 14 cm in width. A large number of old *jōruri* librettos and *sekkyō-bushi* librettos are to be found in this format.

The number of illustrations in *tanrokubon* is not consistent, but most editions have between three and seven full-page illustrations for thirty leaves of printed text. In many *tanrokubon* editions of *Gikeiki* and *Soga Monogatari*, however, there is an usually large number of illustrations, with twelve to fourteen illustrations for thirty to fifty leaves of text. In an eight-volume edition of *Gikeiki*, for example, there are more than a hundred pages of illustrations, and, in a twelve-volume edition of *Soga Monogatari*, more than one hundred and sixty illustrations. The most profusely illustrated *tanrokubon* is a three-volume edition of *Kumano no Honji*, in which one series of illustrations runs through sixteen pages of the book in the style of an *emakimono*.

There is also a variety of styles of interplay between illustrations and calligraphy. As we have seen, full-page illustrations are the most common, with text and illustrations appearing on separate pages. In some *tanrokubon*, however, the illustrations are interspersed in the printed calligraphy in highly complicated patterns. This is the case, for example, in the *yokohon* edition of the old *jōruri* libretto *Takadachi*. Another unusual style is one in which the text is printed in the upper portion of the page and the illustration in the lower portion (for example, *Shishō no Uta-awase*). Even more unusual are *tanrokubon* in which the woodblock for a full-size illustration was cut into a number of pieces that were then employed for details in other illustrations. Some editions of *Soga Monogatari* display this technique and, in *Kanei Gyōkōki*, human figures are used over and over again. In the lavishly illustrated editions of *Gikeiki* and *Soga Monogatari* mentioned above, full-page illustrations are printed on both pages of folded leaves. In a few rare editions, several characters of the text may jut into the lower left or upper right portion of the illustration. Perhaps the most unusual style of pictorial-calligraphic interplay is one in which a series of illustrations continues over several pages in a manner suggestive of narrative picture scrolls. The three-volume edition of *Kumano no Honji* described above is the best example of this style.

In comparison with those of *Nara-ehon*, the covers and bindings of *tanrokubon* are extremely simple. Antique editions are often evaluated on the basis of whether or not they have retained their original covers and title pages. Unfortunately, *tanrokubon* with their original covers are very rare indeed. The *tanrokubon* editions of *Gikeiki* and *Soga Monogatari* retain their original covers because they were sold in sets with protective cases, but these editions are very much the exception. The *tanrokubon* that do have original covers are in extremely poor condition. In a number of cases, the covers have been scribbled on; some are covered with graffiti, and others have been marred by attempts to add color to them. A few covers have been stamped with collectors' seals, but almost all of these seals bear dates after the beginning of the Meiji era. Later in the Edo period, the tendency was for the covers and bindings of books to become increasingly elaborate, but those of *tanrokubon* are extremely simple. The most common original covers are plain indigo or black, and one occasionally sees an orange-red cover.

## THE TOWNSMAN PAINTERS AND THEIR TRADITIONAL STYLES

As is true in the case of early genres of *ukiyo-e*, the craftsmen who created the beautiful styles of *tanrokubon* illustrations remain buried in obscurity. Like the craftsmen who produced *tan-e* and *urushi-e*, they must have been townsman painters (*machi-eshi*) and artisans employed by publishing houses. Despite a great deal of scholarly conjecture, we have not even been able to establish the names of the artists who created the illustrations for the famous *Sagabon* editions of *Ise Monogatari*. It was not until the very end of the Kanbun era (1661–73) that artists such as Yoshida Hanbei in Kyoto and Hishikawa Moronobu in Edo began to sign their book illustration work (although many connoisseurs believe that Hishikawa's woodblock print illustrations are far superior to his paintings, which are all signed).

From the Keichō era through the Kanei era (from 1596 to 1644), the brilliant period of cultural renaissance during which *tanrokubon* enjoyed their great vogue, the custom of signing one's work simply did not exist among townsman artists and craftsmen. Like the dyers who created the lovely textile patterns of the period, the potters who developed new pictorial decorative styles for porcelain, and the artists who established new styles in genre painting, *tanrokubon* illustrators would never have thought of signing their work. Considered in the light of today's "individualism," it all seems strangely remote (and, it strikes me, far from unattractive).

Some tantalizing clues to the identity of the artists and craftsmen of the early Edo period may be gleaned from the history of art schools during the period. Even though, by this time, it had lost one of its greatest masters, Eitoku (1543–90), the Kanō school remained at the zenith of its power and prestige as a result of its continued domination of the Imperial Bureau of Painting (*e-dokoro*). The Chinese Zen styles from which the Kanō styles evolved appealed to the military class, which had adopted Zen as its philosophy and was attempting to assert a cultural identity separate from that of the imperial court. The Chinese painting styles of the Hasegawa school, founded by Hasegawa Tōhaku (1539–1610), and

the Unkoku school, founded by Unkoku Tōgan (1547–1618), were also popular during this period.

The Tosa school of traditional Japanese painting (*Yamato-e*), on the other hand, had been in a state of rapid decline since the beginning of the Muromachi period. It had been briefly revived by Tosa Mitsunobu (1434–1525), but it suffered a further and very serious blow when Mitsunobu's daughter married Kanō Masanobu (1434–1530), founder of the Kanō school. Control of the Imperial Bureau of Painting passed to the Kanō school and the painters of the Tosa school fled to Sakai, where the most famous of them were able to maintain a feeble existence by playing up to members of the flourishing Kanō school. It seems likely that a number of the less fortunate artists were forced to turn to producing *Nara-e* or original paintings for woodblock illustrations.

Certainly, the original paintings for the *Sagabon* editions of *Ise Monogatari* must have been produced by these artists from the Tosa school. There are a number of theories as to the identity of the artist or artists, and Honami Kōetsu, who organized the publishing, is often put forward as a prime candidate. However, in his postscript to the woodblock edition, Nakanoin Michikatsu (1558–1610), a famous scholar and *waka* poet of the period, states that the editions were published "simply to delight the eyes of children with a modicum of taste." Judging from this comment, it seems unlikely that the original paintings were done by an artist of great fame. Nevertheless, the *Sagabon Ise Monogatari* illustrations are executed in a pure Tosa style, and, despite their lack of color, they possess a kind of quiet, unpretentious elegance.

Of course, the *Sagabon* editions are not *tanrokubon* (with the possible exception of the editions I have mentioned on page 15). However, I have in my collection the fragments of what appears to be a *tanrokubon* edition of *Ise Monogatari*. It would make an interesting study to compare the *Sagabon* editions, which were reproductions of Tosa paintings, with this *tanrokubon* edition, in which the painter and the engraver were free to display their skills without the restrictions imposed by the need to copy closely *Yamato-e* originals. Nevertheless, for all the need to abide faithfully by the original paintings, the beauty of the *Sagabon* editions of *Ise Monogatari* is undeniable. That he chose *Yamato-e* for these editions is evidence of Kōetsu's discernment, and of his yearning for the classical refinement of the imperial court. Moreover, the influence of the *Sagabon* editions established an inseparable link between book illustration and *Yamato-e* painting styles. Illustrations of *kōwakamai* librettos, *otogizōshi*, and *kanazōshi*, for example, are almost all in the style of *Yamato-e*.

The anonymous artists and engravers who took part in the creation of *tanrokubon* produced illustrations in a rather stereotyped style, but one that is firmly rooted in the tradition of *Yamato-e*. This style is characterized by such decorative techniques as the use of stylized cloud patterns (*suyari-gasumi*) and a depiction of interior scenes in which portions of walls or ceilings are omitted to afford views of interiors (*fukinuki yatai*)—a style of depiction employed to wonderful effect in the Genji scrolls. Some *tanrokubon* illustrations are free and uninhibited, while others seem so inscrutable as to defy analysis. Some are humorous, and others disingenuously droll, with warriors attired in hunting garb and court ladies in seemingly infinite layers of kimono depicted together in the same scene. Strange though it may seem, these illustrations are very beautiful.

Whatever scenes they chose to depict and whatever styles and techniques they employed, these anonymous painters-turned-woodblock-print-craftsmen created beautiful illustrations. They produced the original paintings for these illustrations with speed and facility; similarly, the engravers apparently did not concern themselves with the subtleties of brush strokes that may have existed in the original paintings. The printed outlines are clear and bold, suggesting that the blocks were engraved with deep, rapid cuts of the engraver's chisel. The engravers must have worked with amazing speed, and yet the finished illustrations possess a protean beauty that emerged spontaneously from their scrupulous observance of a long, established tradition. Certainly, they are heavily influenced by *Yamato-e* painting, but *tanrokubon* illustrations were created in the tradition of Japanese folkcraft, and this is reflected in their execution.

One of the characteristic features of *tanrokubon* illustrations is the heavy exploitation of the *suyari-gasumi* decorative technique, in which stylized cloud patterns intrude into the illustrations in a variety of interesting ways. In some cases, cloud patterns are executed with a few quick strokes, while in other illustrations there has been an attempt at realistic depiction of stratus clouds. One technique employed to achieve this latter effect is the arrangement of cloud patterns over closely drawn horizontal lines (see, for example, *Gikeiki*, page 52). Some authorities suggest that this technique was influenced by Western copperplate prints. Another technique involves the use of cloud patterns to separate two or even three scenes that appear in the same illustration. I suspect that *tanrokubon* illustrators got this idea from the Korean illustrated book *Sankō Gyōjitsu*.

COLORS: CONSIDERING THE COST

*Tanrokubon* illustrations were, of course, colored by hand, and it is the extreme simplicity of their color that accounts for their mysterious beauty. A variety of colors were employed, but orange-red (*tan*) and mineral green (*roku*), from which the books take their name, are typical. Purple (*murasaki*)—actually a reddish brown pigment (*azuki-iro*)—and yellow (*ki*) were also employed extensively, and one occasionally sees indigo, brown, gray, and a light green. It is difficult to believe that the original paintings for these prints were done in only two to four colors. Based on the evidence of early *tanrokubon*, it seems more likely that the artist submitted single-sheet polychrome paintings, perhaps in the style of *Nara-ehon* illustrations. In the case of these early *tanrokubon*, the publishers apparently asked the artisans employed in producing woodblocks and in printing to reproduce the color composition of the original painting.

As the market for *tanrokubon* expanded to include the townsman class, however, publishers attempted to reduce the cost of producing them by employing fewer colors in illustrations. Eventually, the number of colors was reduced to four and, finally, to only two. This had the effect of reducing the price of *tanrokubon* and making them more accessible. The success of this strategy reflects the genius of

these townsman publishers, whose keen sensitivity to the changing tastes of their customers would enable them to dominate literature and art throughout the Edo period.

The colors available to the publishers of the early Edo period were quite different from the artist's oils or watercolors of today, which can be purchased at little cost whenever the artist wants them. The Edo-period publisher had either to purchase the raw materials needed to produce the desired pigments and mix them himself, or employ a craftsman who specialized in producing colors. In either case, it cannot have been an inexpensive undertaking, even for the limited number of colors employed in *tanrokubon*.

Both stylistic analysis of *tanrokubon* illustrations and the history of publishing in this period suggest that colors were applied to the illustrations by members of the publisher's household, including children, apprentices, servants, and other household dependents. Family members would work in teams, with each person responsible for one of two to four colors. Hand-colored devotional prints, such as *Ōtsu-e*, *ema*, and *doro-e* are thought to have been produced in the same way, although it is possible that *tanrokubon* represent the first commercial application of this technique. A variety of techniques were used in applying colors. In some rare cases, color compositions display considerable care, with well-executed shading of one pigment into another. This technique is called *bokashi* and is often used in modern prints. In other illustrations, the colors were applied with bold strokes or simply daubed on by pressing the brush vertically onto the paper. In some cases, these simpler techniques are highly effective, although other illustrations colored in this way are disappointing.

Regardless of technique, *tanrokubon* with a small number of colors are the most beautiful. Indeed, it is perhaps the use of a limited number of colors, and the unsophisticated artistry of the craftsmen who applied them, that accounts for the mysterious subtlety of these later *tanrokubon*. I disagree with those who save their highest praise for *tanrokubon* with the most colors. *Gōtō Kijin* is a good example. Its illustrations have more than ten colors, and yet it is not an outstanding example of *tanrokubon* illustration. Despite the lavish use of colors, the illustrations seem somehow flat and lacking in the fascinating subtlety that one has come to expect from *tanrokubon*. (The oblong *otogizōshi* editions of *Gōtō Kijin* published in Kyoto are exceptions.)

Much the same can be said for the original *tanrokubon* editions of *Otogi Bunko*. (I say "original" because the twenty-three-volume editions of *otogizōshi* published under the same title by Shibukawa Seiemon in Osaka during the Kyōhō era [1716–36] are not *tanrokubon*—see page 28.) A few volumes of *tanrokubon* editions of *Otogi Bunko* published in Kyoto during the Kanei era are extant. Like *Nara-ehon*, these editions were printed on expensive *maniai-gami* paper and have beautiful dark blue covers with flower patterns produced in silver leaf. Titles were printed in the center of the cover in gorgeous reds and gold leaf. Moreover, the illustrations are colored with more than ten pigments. Sumptuous though these editions are, somehow their effect does not approach that of subsequent *tanrokubon*, with their simple illustrations and limited use of colors. Again, this is not so much a result of the artistic weaknesses of the earlier *tanrokubon* illustrations as another reflection of the mysterious power of the less elaborate editions.

*Tanrokubon* illustrations were colored with a bold, unsophisticated hand to produce effects quite unlike anything we have become accustomed to in the modern age. The family members of the publishers of the Edo period were not overly concerned with "staying between the lines," and yet they achieved unparalleled artistic effects that offer an incomparable aesthetic experience to the discerning observer. Like their literary texts, *tanrokubon* illustrations have been disparaged for their crude simplicity, and *tanrokubon* have been valued principally for their rarity and for their importance in the history of woodblock printing. But just as writers and literary scholars have rediscovered the genres of *otogizōshi* and *kōwakamai* librettos, artists, collectors, and art historians have finally begun to turn their attention to *tanrokubon* illustrations.

# III

# *Tanrokubon* As Literature

*TANROKUBON* EDITIONS IN THE CONTEXT OF PUBLISHING

As we have seen, *tanrokubon* were first published at the end of the Genna era (1615–24), reached the height of their popularity in the Kanei era (1624–44), and finally gave way to other types of printed books during the Meireki (1655–58) and Manji (1658–61) eras. Their history thus spans a period of about forty years. In this chapter, I would like to consider the brief history of *tanrokubon* in more detail, with particular attention to the literary genres encompassed by *tanrokubon*.

*Tanrokubon* are treasured today for their rarity, and for their importance in the history of Japanese art and literature. In the period during which they were being published, however, they must have been considered a cheap, insignificant part of the bookseller's repertoire. For this reason, the great majority of extant *tanrokubon* are in poor condition, and it is rare to find *tanrokubon* editions bearing clear colophons identifying the publisher or the date of publication. It is possible, however, to classify them according to literary genre, and, while such a classification is based on criteria pertaining to the history of literature, it is also useful in helping to distinguish between the various characteristic formats of *tanrokubon*.

Tokugawa Ieyasu (1542–1616), who established himself as shogun in 1603, took an active interest in cultural affairs and amassed a huge collection of books and manuscripts. He recognized the importance of developments in print technology and established printing facilities in his castles at Fushimi and Suruga. The printed texts produced at Fushimi and Suruga (*Fushimi-ban* and *Suruga-ban*) were limited, however, to printed editions of the Chinese classics, Japanese literature in Chinese (*kanbun*), and official documents (*komonjo*), a far cry from the popular literary material that formed the subject matter of *tanrokubon*. However, during the two and a half centuries of peace that followed the fall, in 1615, of Osaka Castle, last stronghold of the Toyotomi family, the townsmen became the most powerful cultural force in the land. Their rise to this position of preeminence was rapid, and there is no better testimony of it than the explosive growth of commercial publishing, beginning with the commercial exploitation of movable wooden type technology after the publication of the *Sagabon* editions of *Ise Monogatari*. The *Sagabon* editions were followed by a stream of printed books that quickly developed into a flood. Unlike the Fushimi and Suruga editions, these books were illustrated, employed styles of calligraphy that could be read by people with minimal education, and reproduced Japanese literary texts that appealed to contemporary tastes.

In terms of format and literary content, much the same thing could be said concerning *Nara-ehon*. However, the fact that *Nara-ehon* were produced individually by hand meant that they were extremely expensive, and only people of a very limited class could have afforded them. As a result of advances in printing technology, a relatively large number of copies of an edition could be produced at one time, and it was this development that accounted for the proliferation of books among the townsmen.

The clearest evidence for this is the rapid increase in the number of publishers that occurred during this period. It is thought that the first commercial publishers appeared in the Tenshō era (1573–92). However, they remained quite few in number until the Kanei era, when a period of rapid expansion in publishing activity began that was to transform Japanese society. Professor Inoue Kazuo has documented this expansion in his *Keichō Irai Shoko Shūran* (A Survey of Booksellers from the Keichō Era to the Present).[12] Throughout the twenty-eight-year period between the beginning of the Keichō era (1596) and the beginning of the Kanei era (1624), there were never more than fifteen publishers in Kyoto, the center of publishing activity. However, during the thirty-seven years from the end of the Kanei era (1644) to the Kanbun (1661–73) and Enpō (1673–81) eras, seventy-four new publishing houses had opened in the city.

Moreover, it is quite probable that a good number of publishing houses were not included in Professor Inoue's survey, which is based on publishers' seals. For example, very few of the shops listed in Inoue's study dealt in popular books, despite the large numbers published during the period. With the exception of old *jōruri* librettos and *sekkyō-bushi* librettos, most popular editions do not have dates in the publisher's seal. Either that, or they do not have a publisher's seal at all. It seems likely therefore that a number of publishers who dealt in these editions were overlooked. If so, there must have been many more publishers active in Kyoto during the period.

It must be emphasized that, unlike *Nara-ehon*, which were produced in all of the country's major urban centers, all *tanrokubon* were published in Kyoto. There are no extant *tanrokubon* bearing publishers' seals indicating that they were published in Edo or Osaka. One can say with certainty that books with color illustrations printed in Edo or Osaka during this period are not *tanrokubon*. Any collector presented with such an edition should approach it with extreme care. In some cases, colors may have been added by the original owner in a whimsical attempt to imitate the *tanrokubon* popular in Kyoto or, perhaps, for more dubious purposes. In most cases, however, these books are simply fakes.

What classes of people bought *tanrokubon*? Even before the Edo period, the dance theater *kōwakamai* had been popular among the powerful warrior families surrounding Oda Nobunaga (1534–82), and Nobunaga himself once performed a *kōwakamai* before launching a major campaign. The puppet theaters—old *jōruri* and *sekkyō-bushi*—had been admitted even into the imperial court. With this historical background, there is no doubt that *tanrokubon*, which contained illustrated texts of the librettos for these popular performance arts and other genres of popular

literature, were purchased merely for the women and children of great court and warrior families during the early Edo period. Certainly they were widely enjoyed by priests and nuns and other members of the Buddhist establishment. However, it was during this period that the enormous energy and economic power of the townsman class exploded into the cultural sphere, and there is no question that it was among the townsmen, whose tastes and lifestyles were unencumbered by the demands of high scholarship, that amakihon found their widest audience.

## CLASSIFICATION BY LITERARY GENRE

The literary genres encompassed by amakihon are essentially the same as those of Nara-ehon and they present similar problems. There is as yet no consensus on definitions of these genres, and many scholars would deal with all texts and amakihon texts, as noted above. Given the recent interest in Japanese performance arts and the fact that individual genres are often given characteristic treatment, with annotation editions, I believe that such an approach only serves to obscure important issues of literary and art history. I have classified tanrokubon editions according to the following seven literary genres. In addition, I have added two categories to distinguish tanrokubon editions of emakimono and editions produced with the technique of movable wooden type.

1. Tanrokubon editions of classical tale literature (ko-monogatari).
2. Tanrokubon editions of war tales (gunki monogatari).
3. Tanrokubon editions of Kowakamai libretti.
4. Tanrokubon editions of nō plays.
5. Tanrokubon editions of kyōgen.
6. Tanrokubon editions of ukiyo-zōshi libretti.
7. Tanrokubon editions of old print libretti.
8. Tanrokubon editions of picture scrolls (emakimono).
9. Movable wooden type editions of tanrokubon (ko-katsuji).

### 1. Tanrokubon Editions of Classical Tale Literature

There is only a single edition of what I have called "classical tale literature" among tanrokubon. Moreover, as I mentioned on page 20, there is some question whether to emphasize that this is a true tanrokubon edition, or whether it belongs among the sashi-e editions of ko-monogatari. As the only extant edition of its kind, this text is extremely important for our study of the history of tanrokubon and their relationship to other types of books.

### 2. Tanrokubon Editions of War Tales

War tales, or gunki monogatari, belong to a genre of Japanese literature that encompasses the romantic, highly lyrical war tales written during the Kamakura period, such as Heike Monogatari, Hōgen Monogatari, and Heiji Monogatari, as well as the popular tales of heroism and adventure written during the Muromachi period, such as Taiheiki, Gikeiki, and Soga Monogatari. There are only a few tanrokubon editions of the complete texts of war tales, and these should be carefully distinguished from editions of emakimono that deal with the same themes and the same heroes.

literature, were purchased secretly for the women and children of great court and warrior families during the early Edo period. Certainly they were widely enjoyed by priests and nuns and other members of the Buddhist establishment. However, it was during this period that the enormous energy and economic power of the townsman class exploded into the cultural sphere, and there is no question that it was among the townsmen, whose tastes and lifestyles were unencumbered by the demands of high social status, that *tanrokubon* found their widest audience.

CLASSIFICATION BY LITERARY GENRE

The literary genres encompassed by *tanrokubon* are essentially the same as those of *Nara-ehon*, and they present similar problems. There is as yet no consensus on definitions of these genres, and many scholars would deal with all *Nara-ehon* and *tanrokubon* texts as *otogizōshi*.[13] Given the recent interest in Japanese performance arts and the fact that individual genres are often given characteristic treatment in *tanrokubon* editions, I believe that such an approach only serves to obscure important issues of literary and art history. I have classified *tanrokubon* editions according to the following seven literary genres. In addition, I have added two categories to distinguish *tanrokubon* editions of *emakimono* and editions produced with the technique of movable wooden type.

1. *Tanrokubon* editions of classical tale literature (*ko-monogatari*).
2. *Tanrokubon* editions of war tales (*gunki monogatari*).
3. *Tanrokubon* editions of *kōwakamai* librettos.
4. *Tanrokubon* editions of *otogizōshi*.
5. *Tanrokubon* editions of *kanazōshi*.
6. *Tanrokubon* editions of *sekkyō-bushi* librettos.
7. *Tanrokubon* editions of old *jōruri* librettos.
8. *Tanrokubon* editions of picture scrolls (*emakimono*).
9. Movable wooden type editions of *tanrokubon* (*ko-katsujibon*).

## 1. *Tanrokubon* Editions of Classical Tale Literature

There is only one extant *tanrokubon* edition of what I have called "classical tale literature," the illustrated version of *Ise Monogatari* that I mentioned on page 20. I have established this classification in order to emphasize that this is a true *tanrokubon* edition and to separate it clearly from the *Sagabon* editions of *Ise Monogatari*. As the only extant edition of its kind, this text is extremely important for our study of the history of *tanrokubon* and their relationship to other types of books.

## 2. *Tanrokubon* Editions of War Tales

War tales, or *gunki monogatari*, belong to a genre of Japanese literature that encompasses the romantic, highly lyrical war tales written during the Kamakura period, such as *Hōgen Monogatari*, *Heiji Monogatari*, and *Heike Monogatari*, as well as the popular tales of heroism and adventure written during the Muromachi period, such as *Taiheiki*, *Gikeiki*, and *Soga Monogatari*. There are only a few *tanrokubon* editions of the complete texts of war tales, and these should be carefully distinguished from editions of *otogizōshi* that deal with the same themes and the same heroes.

For example, *Gikeiki* is quite different from *otogizōshi* that draw their material from the original tale or from other legendary accounts of Yoshitsune.[14] The war tales are longer than other genres of *tanrokubon*; the *tanrokubon* editions of *Gikeiki* have eight volumes and those of *Soga Monogatari* have twelve. Moreover, the editions of war tales are much more heavily illustrated and more carefully produced in general than is usual for *tanrokubon*. Indeed, the *tanrokubon* editions of war tales are particularly beautiful and are considered to be rare masterpieces.

There is a single-sheet print, *Ōsaka Abe no Kassen*, in which colors have been added to the printed illustration by hand. It bears a publisher's seal that reads, "Fifth month, Keichō 20" (1615). I have not included it in the list of *tanrokubon* editions of war tales on page 199 because it is a single-sheet print and because it was printed with the technique of *kawara-zuri*. There are also two interesting sets of scrolls produced in 1626. These are described below in the section on picture scrolls.

### 3. *Tanrokubon* Editions of *Kōwakamai* Librettos

*Kōwakamai* is a dance theater that evolved from *kusemai*, which was one of the popular entertainments performed at temple gates during the Muromachi period and which exerted a strong influence on the performance techniques of Nō. During the period of almost constant warfare preceding the Edo period, referred to variously as the Warring States or the Azuchi–Momoyama period (1573–1603), *kōwakamai* developed into a stage art patronized by the ruling warrior elite surrounding first Oda Nobunaga and subsequently Toyotomi Hideyoshi. It takes its name from the performer who is traditionally held to be its originator, Momonoi Naoaki of Echizen, whose childhood name, and perhaps his stage name too, was Kōwaka Maru. Kōwaka Maru formed a troupe of traveling performers who performed dance plays based on legends related to the war tales described above.

As *kōwakamai* developed into a stage art with powerful patronage, two separate traditions developed. The *kōwaka-ryū*, which traces its history back to Kōwaka Maru, is performed by two performers, while the *daikashira-ryū*, founded by Jirōzaemon Naoyoshi of Yamato, is performed by three performers. The latter may still be seen in the village of Ōe in Fukuoka Prefecture.

The term *kōwakamai* librettos (*kōwaka bukyoku* or *mai no hon*) refers to the printed or written texts of the plays denuded of musical and recitational neumes. These texts were probably read as fictional narratives in much the same manner as *otogizōshi*, and, for this reason, some scholars believe that they should be dealt with as *otogizōshi*. Such a treatment, however, ignores their importance in the history of Japanese performance arts and the consequences for the texts themselves of their association with performance. There seem to have been thirty-six titles in the original repertoire, but more than ten additional titles are known to be extant in written or printed texts. These additional titles are called *bangaimono*. All of the *kōwakamai* librettos draw their fictional content from war tales and related stories and legends. This fact, as well as the bold performance styles of *kōwakamai*, probably accounts for their popularity among the warrior elite.[15]

### 4. *Tanrokubon* Editions of *Otogizōshi*

The term *otogizōshi* refers to a genre of literature written during the Muromachi

and Momoyama periods and the early part of the Edo period. The term itself, as well as the definition of the genre, is the subject of much scholarly debate, and a number of alternative designations have been suggested: Muromachi period tales (*Muromachi jidai monogatari*), Muromachi period books (*Muromachi jidai zōshi*), Muromachi period novels (*Muromachi jidai shōsetsu*), late medieval novels (*kinko shōsetsu*), medieval novels (*chūsei shōsetsu*), and so on.[16] I have used the term to refer to a repertoire of approximately three hundred titles. Before the Edo period, *otogizōshi* became the texts for *Nara-ehon* and other hand-written editions. During the early Edo period, they were a major source of texts for *tanrokubon* and other types of printed books.

The search for the origins of the term *otogizōshi* has provided folklorists and literary historians with one of their most interesting puzzles. The term itself was probably coined in the Kyōhō era (1716–36) by the Osaka publisher Shibukawa Seiemon, who published oblong woodblock editions of twenty-three *otogizōshi* under the titles *Otogi Bunko* and *Otogizōshi*. These editions of *otogizōshi* are close-ly related to a special subcategory of *tanrokubon*, *tanrokubon* editions of *otogizōshi* in an oblong book (*yokohon*) format.

The last volumes of the Shibukawa editions of *Otogi Bunko* and *Otogizōshi* bear a publisher's seal that reads, "The Glade of Books, Shibukawa Seiemon's shop in Junkei-machi near Shinsai Bridge" (*Shorin Shinsai-bashi Junkei-machi no Shibukawa Seiemon*). Unfortunately, the seal does not include the date of publication. Accor-ding to Inoue Kazuo's *Keichō Irai Shoko Shūran*, Shibukawa's shop in Osaka was called Kashiwabaraya and was open for business from the Enpō era (1673–81) until the Keiō era (1865–68). The Shibukawa editions are oblong woodblock printed books without color illustrations.

There are, however, early woodblock-printed editions in the same format as *Otogi Bunko* that were printed on *maniai-gami* and hand-colored with red (*beni*), orange-red, indigo (*ao*), pale flesh-tone pigments (*usu-momo iro*), green, white, yellow, brown (*cha iro*), and even silver. These editions were probably sold originally as sets containing all twenty-three stories. Some scholars argue that these editions were published during the Kanbun era (1661–73), but my own research suggests that they were published during the Kanei era (1624–44). It seems likely, therefore, that the first *Otogi Bunko* and *Otogizōshi* editions were *tanrokubon* with color applied by hand and that they were first published in Kyoto during the Kanei era. I believe that Shibukawa obtained the original woodblocks for these editions sometime during the Kyōhō era, probably in 1716. By that time, the practice of applying colors to woodblock-printed illustrations was no longer popular, so the Shibukawa editions were sold as monochrome printed books.

An oblong *tanrokubon* edition in three volumes of *Bunshō Sōshi*, the first story in the Shibukawa editions, survives in the collection of the Japan Folk Art Museum (it belonged originally to the collection of the late Professor Yokoyama Shigeru). This edition is in extraordinarily good condition, with original covers and title papers. Also preserved in the collection of the Japan Folk Art Museum is a beautiful edition of the second volume of a three-volume oblong *tanrokubon* edition of *Bunshō Sōshi,* The publisher's seal in this edition reads, ''Shichibei of the Yamagataya bookstore in Tsūkobashi-chō, Nijō [Kyoto]'' (*Nijō Tsūkobashi-chō Yamagataya Shichibei*). This provides positive evidence that early oblong *tanrokubon* editions of *Otogi Bunko* were published in Kyoto and not in Osaka. These oblong *tanrokubon* editions are extremely rare, and, besides the two editions already mentioned, only seven other examples are extant.

## 5. *Tanrokubon* Editions of *Kanazōshi*

The term *kanazōshi* is quite old, and it seems to have been used originally as the designation for any book (*sōshi*) in which the text is written in Japanese as opposed to *kanbun*, a style of writing in which the text is written in classical Chinese but read in Japanese. The word *kana* refers simply to the native Japanese syllabaries, *hiragana* and *katakana*. Thus, *kanazōshi* referred to books, as opposed to scrolls (*makimono*), written in Japanese, as opposed to *kanbun*. For example, the term was apparently used in this way in one section of a catalogue of books and scrolls published during the Kanbun era under the title *Washo narabi ni Kana-rui* (Japanese Manuscripts and Things Written in *Kana*). Texts classified as *kanazōshi* in this catalogue include a popular genre of didactic and instructional texts, guides to famous places (*meishoki*), the legends of famous temples and shrines (*honji* or *engi*), and "critiques" of popular actors, plays, and courtesans (*hyōbanki*).

Today, however, scholars use the term to refer to texts of fictional narrative considered to be transitional from true *otogizōshi* of the Muromachi period to the *ukiyozōshi* of the Edo period, a genre that is considered to have begun with the publication of Ihara Saikaku's *Kōshoku Ichidai Otoko* (The Man Who Loved Love) in 1685. *Tanrokubon* editions of *kanazōshi* are very rare. *Usuyuki Monogatari* and *Shichinin Bikuni* (pp. 178–186) are representative of the genre.[17]

## 6. *Tanrokubon* Editions of *Sekkyō-bushi* Librettos

Like *kōwakamai*, *sekkyō-bushi* was not originally a stage art, but it developed at the end of the Kamakura period or the beginning of the Muromachi period as a form of oral recitation performed by priests and nuns of low rank who were involved in evangelical work among the lower classes. These wandering priests and nuns sometimes became famous in their own right, and the lives and adventures of Ikkyū Shōnin, Ippen Shōnin, and the nuns of Kumano themselves became the subjects of *sekkyō-bushi*, as well as of *jōruri*, *otogizōshi*, and other genres of popular literature.

*Sekkyō-bushi* began to evolve as a performance art before *jōruri*, but the process of its development is similar in many ways. During the Keichō era (1596–1615), *sekkyō-bushi* performers began to stage performances employing a type of puppet that could be manipulated (*ayatsuri ningyō*). This, together with increasingly sophisticated chanting styles, culminated in the perfection of a new stage art that enjoyed immense popularity during the Kanei era and continued to attract a large following for at least the next thirty years.

Like *kōwakamai* and old *jōruri* librettos, *sekkyō-bushi* librettos were hand-copied (*Nara-ehon*) or printed (*tanrokubon*) versions of the stories that were chanted orally in performances. These were read as narrative fiction, and some scholars believe that they should be considered as one type of *otogizōshi*. Again, I have based my own research on a more closely defined classification. Only five *tanrokubon* edi-

tions of *sekkyō-bushi* librettos are known to be extant, one old movable type edition and four woodblock editions. Even among *tanrokubon*, these editions are unusual for their crude simplicity. All of the extant editions are roughly colored by hand with only the two colors orange-red and mineral green.[18]

## 7. *Tanrokubon* Editions of Old *Jōruri* Librettos

*Jōruri* had been perfected as a performance art comprising all the elements of *jōruri* as it is performed today by the end of the Keichō era (1596–1615). Its development was the result of an extraordinary process of creative synthesis that culminated in a completely new art form. As in modern *jōruri*, or Bunraku, this synthesis involved a mixture of puppet theater, *jōruri* chanting, and the *shamisen* as a musical accompaniment. The puppet theater and *jōruri* chanting styles had existed since the Muromachi period and had undergone a steady evolution toward increased sophistication. In the case of *jōruri*, this included the development of a wide dramaturgical repertoire. The *shamisen* was the new element. The now familiar *shamisen* was a new musical instrument at this time, developed in the sixteenth and seventeenth centuries by improving on the *jabisen*, a musical instrument imported from the Ryūkyū Islands. It was probably first exploited in the evolving *jōruri* theater.

The *jōruri* theater (*jōruri ayatsuri shibai*) continued to develop new styles and additions to its repertoire. However, I consider the period of about seventy-five years between the late Keichō era and Jōkyō 1 (1684) to be the period of "old *jōruri*." It was in 1684 that Chikamatsu Monzaemon, the extraordinary dramaturgist who revolutionized the *jōruri* theater, wrote his first librettos for Uji Kadayū and Takemoto Gidayū. All *tanrokubon* editions of *jōruri* librettos belong to the earlier tradition of old *jōruri*. Compared to other literary genres, *tanrokubon* editions of old *jōruri* librettos are fairly numerous, and a large number of them bear publisher seals indicating the date of their publication.[19]

## 8. *Tanrokubon* Picture Scrolls

As is true in the case of *Nara-ehon*, there is some debate as to whether picture scrolls (*emakimono*) should be included in a discussion of illustrated books (*ehon* or *e-zōshi*). In the case of *tanrokubon*, however, there are only two extant examples of scrolls printed in the style of *tanrokubon*. Without entering the debate over whether these scrolls should be included in a strict classification of *tanrokubon*, I will describe them briefly.

*Kanei Gyōkōki* (An Imperial Procession of the Kanei Era) is a set of three scrolls printed in the style of *tanrokubon* that depict the procession of Emperor Go-Mizunoo to the shogun's Nijō palace in the Kanei era. *Gion Sairei Gyōretsu E-maki* (Picture Scroll of the Gion Festival) survives in sixteen fragments discovered inside the thick cover binding an eight-volume *tanrokubon* edition of *Gikeiki* published in 1635. An examination of these fragments revealed that the scrolls depicted the procession of a Gion festival held sometime during the Kanei era.

## 9. Movable Wooden Type Editions of *Tanrokubon*

For a short period from the Keichō (1596–1615) to the Kanei (1624–44) era, books printed by exploiting the new techniques of movable wooden type enjoyed an extraordinary vogue, to the extent that woodblock editions (*seihan*) were published only on rare occasions. Modern scholars refer to these books as *ko-katsujibon*, or "editions printed with old movable type," in order to distinguish them from copperplate printing. A number of *tanrokubon* editions were produced with this technique.

Early movable wooden type printing was achieved by engraving one *kana* syllable onto each block of wooden type. Later, techniques were developed in which two, three, or even four *kana* syllables written in cursive calligraphy could be engraved onto each block of wooden type. Most *tanrokubon* printed in this format have ten to twelve lines of text on each page with twenty to twenty-two *kana* syllables in each line. Small wooden blocks upon which illustrations had been engraved were employed in much the same way as the small blocks of wooden type. For example, in an edition of *Kanei Gyōkōki* printed with movable type, human figures, horses, and palanquins that appear in one illustration are used over and over again in subsequent illustrations. The illustrations in this edition are not colored, and it cannot be considered to be a *tanrokubon*. However, one *tanrokubon* edition does exist in which a reproduction of the earlier movable wooden type edition was produced with the printing process called *kabuse-bori*, in which a woodblock is prepared by employing a print produced with movable wooden type printing to engrave an exact copy on the woodblock. This process was also used in preparing new woodblocks after the original woodblock had worn out after repeated printings.

A woodblock edition of *Kōya Daishi Gyōjō Zuga* in which the illustrations have been employed in the same way was published in 1596. There are also editions of *Soga Monogatari* in which full-page illustrations were divided into four parts, with each of the smaller parts employed subsequently in later sections of the text. One result of the practice of employing the technique of *kabuse-bori* to produce woodblock copies of *tanrokubon* printed with movable type is that the woodblock edition may appear to be an edition printed with movable wooden type. This demands special care on the part of scholars and collectors, and it has resulted in a number of unfortunate mistakes.

# ✣ IV ✣

# The Term *Tanrokubon*

OLDEST REFERENCES TO A MODERN COINAGE

Unlike such terms as *tan-e* or *beni-e*, designations for prints in early genres of *ukiyo-e* coined simultaneously with the creations of the genres themselves,[20] the term *tanrokubon* does not appear until the end of the Meiji era (1868–1912) or, perhaps, the beginning of the Taishō era (1912–26). Before Meiji, these books seem to have been called *edoribon*, as in Ryūtei Tanehiko's *Yōshabako* (see page 11), or *saishikibon*.

It is important at this early stage in modern scholarship on *tanrokubon* to investigate the process by which the term itself gained currency among scholars and collectors. When did the term *edoribon* give way to *tanrokubon*? In his *Ehon no Kenkyū* (A Study of Picture Books), Nakada Katsunosuke has followed the work of Miyazaki Harumi[21] in asserting that "the term *tanrokubon* was first used after the beginning of the Taishō era."[22] My own research, however, suggests that the term may have been coined in the Meiji era.

One piece of evidence to support my theory is found in the first issue of *Garakuta Bunko*, the literary magazine established by the Kenyūsha in May 1885. The Kenyūsha, or Society of Friends of the Inkstone, was formed in 1885 by Ozaki Kōyō, Ishibashi Shian, and a number of other influential Meiji-era writers and artists. In Ishibashi's manifesto introducing the new journal, we find the following:

> We great talents, sharing similar tastes, have banded together . . . determined to take up the writing brush and produce our own work. Our calligraphy is executed in the ancient Chinese styles—most difficult to read. Our pictures, in the *tanroku* style, are artless—even childlike. Precisely for these reasons, these writings will undoubtedly become treasured playthings.

I am convinced that Ishibashi's "pictures in the *tanroku* style" refers to *tanrokubon*.

The oldest explicit reference to *tanrokubon* is found in Mizutani Futō's *Bungei Hyakka Zensho* (Complete Reference Encyclopedia of Literary Arts), published in 1910 (Meiji 43). His entry for *edoribon* reads as follows: "These books are called *edoribon* and also *tanrokubon*."[23]

It is true, however, that what we now call *tanrokubon* were not widely known by that designation even by the time Mizutani published his *Bungei Hyakka Zensho*. The following is an excerpt from a personal correspondence from Okimori Naosaburō (received on 14 May 1970). Okimori, who later became owner of

Okimori Shoten in Osaka, worked in the famous Osaka bookstore Shikada Shōundō in the years 1907 through 1912:

> During the period when I was working in the Osaka shop [Shōundō], they were all called *edoribon*. We did not call them *tanrokubon*, and, at that time, people would not have understood the word. It would have been easier to understand *tanroku-eiribon*. . . . In the Meiji 40s [1907–1912], we did use such words as *tanroku-eiri* and *tanroku-saiiri*. Also, based on my recollection of what I heard personally during the period, the word *tanroku-eiribon* was used only in reference to *tanrokubon* published during the Kanei era [1624–44]. Finally, people began to shorten *tanroku-eiribon* to *tanrokubon*.

Fortunately, a complete set of Shikada Shōundō's catalogues of rare books, which were published monthly beginning in 1890, is preserved in the library of Keiō University.[24] An examination of these catalogues has enabled me to trace the shifts in terms used to designate what we now call *tanrokubon*. For example, in May 1903, Shōundō published a catalogue for an exhibition of old printed books in which four *tanrokubon* were on display and one other rare *tanrokubon* was offered for sale. They were described as follows:

1. *Ongyōkō Shidai* [An Imperial Procession of the Kanei Era]. Published during the Kanei era. In the style of *Kanei Gyōkōki Gyōretsu E-maki* [Picture Scroll Depicting an Imperial Procession of the Kanei Era]. Includes a short introduction. *Iro-dori saishiki* [illustrations colored by hand]. Offered by Shōundō.

2. *Hōgen–Heiji Monogatari* [The Tale of Hōgen and the Tale of Heiji]. Published in the sixth month of Kanei 3 [1626]. Woodblock-printed *kana* text and illustrations. *Tanshoku-dori* [hand-colored with orange-red], with an orange-red [*tan*] cover. Offered by Shōundō.

3. *Shishō no Uta-awase: Mushi, Tori, Sakana, Kedamono* [Poetry Contest of the Four Living Things: Crawling Creatures, Birds, Sea Creatures, Beasts]. *Kokatsujibon* [old movable wooden type edition]. *Tanshoku-dori* [hand-colored with orange-red]. Offered by Shōundō.

4. *Sannin Hōshi* [Three Buddhist Sages]. Published in the Meireki era [1655–58]. *Irodori-eiri* [includes hand-colored illustrations]. Offered by Mr. Tomioka of Kyoto.

5. (For sale) *Hōgen–Heiji Monogatari*. Published in the Kanei era. Excellent edition with original orange-red covers. *Tanshokudori-bon* [block-printed illustrations hand-colored with orange-red]. Six volumes. 4 yen.

As may be seen from the above, the term *edoribon* was not being used by Shōundō in 1903. We see instead such designations as *eiri tanshoku-dori* (printed illustrations hand-colored with orange-red), *iro-dori saishiki* (illustrations colored by hand), and *ehon tanshoku-dori* (picture book, illustrations hand-colored with orange-red). The term *tanshoku-dori* (hand-colored with orange-red) was undoubtedly designed to suggest the *tan-e* (orange-red prints) genre of *ukiyo-e* prints, which were popular during the Kanei era. These single-sheet prints also featured woodblock-printed illustrations with orange-red and other colors applied by hand.

A closer examination of Shōundō's monthly catalogues reveals that *tanrokubon* were already rare by the time the catalogues were published and provides further evidence concerning the evolution of the term *tanrokubon*. The following entries have been identified as *tanrokubon*:

Issue No. 76, September 1910 (Meiji 43)
*Manjū. Mai no hon* [*kōwakamai* libretto]. *Edoribon*. Second volume only. 1 yen 50 sen.

Issue No. 79, October 1913 (Taishō 2)
*Sazare-ishi* [The Tale of Empress Sazareishi]. *Otogibon* [*Otogizōshi*]. *Saiga-iri* [color illustrations]. Seven leaves (fourteen pages). Oblong book [*yokohon*]. One volume. 1 yen 50 sen.

Issue No. 80, October·1914 (Taishō 3)
*Kagekiyo. Kōwakamai no hon* [*kōwakamai libretto*]. Second volume only. Published in the Meireki era [1655–58]. *Tanrokubon*. Large upright book. 5 yen.

Issue No. 81, August 1915 (Taishō 4)
*Yashima* [Yoshitsune on Yashima]. *Kōwakamai no hon* [*kōwakamai* libretto]. Published in the Meireki era. *Tanroku-edoribon* [illustrated with *tanroku-e*]. Page leaves reinforced. One volume. 3 yen 50 sen. *Taishokukan. Mai no hon* [*Kōwakamai* libretto]. Published in the Keian era [1648–52]. *Tanrokubon*. 1 yen 20 sen.

Issue No. 85, July 1917 (Taishō 6)
*Soga Monogatari* [The Tale of the Soga]. Published in Shōhō 3 [1646]. Illustrated in the classical style. *Tanroku-edoribon*. Twelve volumes. 10 yen.

Issue No. 87, September 1919 (Taishō 8)
*Saru Genji* [Monkey Genji]. *Nara-e tai edoribon* [*edoribon* in the style of *Nara-ehon*]. An extremely rare edition with original cover and title paper illustrated in the classical style. Engraved titles. Oblong book. 18 yen.

Issue No. 95, October 1922 (Taishō 11)
*Gikeiki* [The Chronicle of Yoshitsune]. *Tanrokubon*. Published in the Shōhō era [1644–48]. An *edoribon* in the classical style. Volumes 1, 2, 3, and 8. Four volumes. 10 yen.

Issue No. 97, October 1923 (Taishō 12)
*Kumano no Honji* [The Legend of Kumano]. Published in the Kanei era. *Tanroku-edoribon*. Repaired in numerous places. Two volumes re-bound into one. One volume. 10 yen.
*Kōbō Daishi Gohonji* [The Legend of Kōbō Daishi]. Published in the Kanei era. A classical *e-maki* [picture scroll]. The first two volumes are original *tanrokubon*. The third is a hand-copied and hand-illustrated imitation of the original *tanrokubon*. Three-volume set. 15 yen.

Issue No. 98, September 1924 (Taishō 13)
*Taishokukan* [The Story of the Taishokukan]. *Mai no hon* [*kōwakamai* libretto]. *Tanrokubon*. One folded leaf [two pages of text and illustration] missing. One volume. 20 yen.

As may be seen from these entries, Shōundō used the term *tanrokubon* in their catalogue for the first time in 1914, but they continued to use such terms as *tanroku-edoribon* up to the end of the Taishō era.

Similarly, the famous Osaka bookstore Sugimoto Ryōkōdō published the first issue of its catalogue, *Koten to Nishiki-e Mokuroku* (Catalogue of Classical Editions and *Nishiki-e*), in 1925 (Taishō 14). An examination of this catalogue reveals that they were still using the term *edoribon* (for a *tanrokubon* entitled *Tsukimitsu no Sōshi*). However, in the second issue for 1926 (Shōwa 2), we find the term *tanrokubon* (in an entry for an edition of *Soga Monogatari*). Thus, Mizutani Futō's use of the term in his Meiji-era encyclopedia is apparently a rather special case, and it seems that it was not until the beginning of the Taishō era that the term was widely used among art lovers. Moreover, such terms as *edoribon* continued to enjoy currency until the end of the era in 1926.

This raises the interesting question of who it was that coined the term *tanrokubon*. Is the term an abbreviation for *tanroku-eiribon*, as Okimori suggests? Or was it in fact Mizutani Futō himself who first used the term? It is difficult to say.

There is an interesting theory that *tanrokubon* were originally called *sanshokubon* (three-color books). This theory was advanced in the journal of the Kisho Fukusei Kai (Society for the Reproduction of Rare Books and Manuscripts), in an article on a *tanrokubon* entitled *Mushi no Uta-awase* (The Insects' Poetry Contest):

> Finally, the techniques of illustrating popular literature developed to the point that the three colors orange-red, mineral green, and yellow were being applied to block-printed illustrations by hand. These books were called *tanrokubon* or *sanshokubon*.

I have never seen the term *sanshokubon* used in reference to *tanrokubon* anywhere else. I suspect that this idea was based on an incorrect reading of the following passage from Mizutani's *Kanazōshi*:

> The fact is that the yellow pigments employed in the books [*sanshokubon*] colored with the three colors orange-red, mineral green, and yellow were intended to imitate the gold foil employed in *Nara-ehon*.[25]

In fact, of course, Mizutani used the term *sanshokubon* quite casually, and had no intention of suggesting it as an alternative term for *tanrokubon*.

This survey of the various theories and the evidence concerning the origins of the term *tanrokubon* suggests that it was probably being used by the end of the Meiji era but did not gain wide currency among scholars and collectors until sometime in the Taishō era. Moreover, it suggests the need for extreme care in using historical references in any attempt to authenticate individual editions. *Tanrokubon* are extremely rare, and it is unusual to find editions with clear colophons. Often, they can be authenticated only by an expert.

# *Tanrokubon* Illustrations and Synopses of the Texts

# A Classical Tale

## (*Ko-monogatari*)

## 古物語

# Ise Monogatari

伊 勢 物 語

## Tales of Ise

Kanei-era (1624–44) edition. Large upright book. Second volume (fragment) of two. Ten illustrations, approximately 19.0 cm by 14.0 cm. (For a complete English translation, see Helen McCullough, *Tales of Ise: Lyrical Episodes from Tenth Century Japan* [Stanford, Calif.: Stanford University Press, 1968].)

*This edition of the* Ise Monogatari *is the only extant* tanrokubon *edition of a literary work from the Heian period. The* Ise Monogatari *itself, which is thought to have been completed in its present form in the period between the late ninth and early tenth centuries, was already a classic by the time Murasaki Shikibu began* The Tale of Genji. *It revolutionized the genre of* monogatari *in much the same way that the* Kokinshū *transformed the genre of classical court poetry (*waka*), and it was the first* monogatari *to break out of the tradition of tale literature and assume some of the characteristics of a novel.*

*The novel is dominated by pre-Kokinshū poems from the oeuvre of Ariwara no Narihira (825–80), one of the most famous poets of the Kokinshū. Therefore, it is considered to be the first, and the most outstanding, work in the genre called* uta monogatari, *or poem tales. Later Heian-period writers believed that the Ise Monogatari had been written by Narihira himself, and this traditional theory of the authorship of the novel was accepted by modern scholars until quite recently. Unfortunately, textual studies carried out since World War Two have demonstrated that the text could not have been written during Narihira's lifetime.*

*Although the novel's main character is identified only as "a man of old," there is little doubt that he is indeed Narihira. The narrative structure of the novel is similar to that of the thirty poems by Narihira in the Kokinshū together with their prose introductions (*kotobagaki*), and it has been suggested that a separate collection of these later poems could be considered a second Ise Monogatari. In the Ise Monogatari itself, however, Narihira becomes a fictional character representing the ideal man of the Heian period. The poetry is, of course, love poetry, and, though all the poems were written by Narihira, they are often put into the mouths of the various women encountered by "the man of old." It is this element of fiction that sets the Ise Monogatari apart from the collection of Narihira's Kokinshū poems and, indeed, from almost everything that preceded it. While the female characters in the novel are given many different names or titles, recent interpretations suggest that, in fact, there is a central female character, corresponding to Lady Murasaki in The Tale of Genji. Similarly, studies of allusion in The Tale of Genji have revealed that the Ise Monogatari had an enormous influence on the later novel. The Ise Monogatari had become a classic by the time of the publication of the tanrokubon edition, but, as was true of the other great works of Japanese literature, the woodblock edition may have provided the first chance for a wide range of people to read it.*

# War Tales

*(Gunki Monogatari)*

軍記物語

# Hōgen Monogatari 保元物語
## The Tale of Hōgen

Three chapters (*maki*). Kanei-era (1624–44) edition. Large upright book. One volume (chapter one) extant. Illustrations approximately 20.0 cm by 15.5 cm.

**Chapter One**: Emperor Toba abdicates in favor of his first son, who becomes Emperor Sutoku. However, Bifukumon-in, the ex-emperor's favorite consort, unexpectedly bears him a male child. When this child reaches the age of two, Toba forces Sutoku to abdicate in his favor, and the child assumes the throne as Emperor Konoe. Konoe dies suddenly in his sixteenth year, and Sutoku now hopes to regain control of the throne by making Prince Ichinomiya Shigeto emperor. Toba ignores his wishes once again. At the behest of Bifukumon-in, he arranges to have Prince Shinomiya Go-Shirakawa succeed Konoe instead, thereby further inflaming Sutoku's resentment.

Paralleling these events in the imperial family, relations break down between Fujiwara no Yorinaga, the minister of the left, and his elder brother Tadamichi, the regent. Yorinaga's dislike of his elder brother, with whom he has long shared a relationship similar to that between Sutoku and his father, finally leads him to side with Sutoku in his attempt to make Prince Shigeto emperor.

With the death of ex-Emperor Toba on the twelfth day of the seventh month of 1156, Sutoku's prestige as ex-emperor is greatly enhanced, and Yorinaga joins him openly. Together they persuade such powerful warriors as Minamoto no Tameyoshi, his son Hachirō Tametomo, and Taira no Tadamasa to join them in plotting a coup d'état. Well aware of these developments, Go-Shirakawa solicits the support of warriors such as Minamoto no Yoshitomo and Taira no Kiyomori, and the stage is set for a military clash between Emperor Go-Shirakawa and ex-Emperor Sutoku.

Both sides hold councils of war, but with quite different results. In Sutoku's war council, Minamoto no Tametomo, who is famous for his martial valor, proposes a night attack but is overruled by Yorinaga. Minamoto no Yoshitomo, the leader of Go-Shirakawa's allies, has the same idea, and his proposal is accepted. Thus in the early dawn of the eleventh day of the seventh month, Yoshitomo, Kiyomori, and their retainers attack Sutoku's Shirakawa palace.

**Chapter Two**: Under surprise attack, the warriors at Shirakawa palace display heroic bravery, and a barrage of arrows launched by Tametomo, an archer of almost supernatural skill and ferocity, drives the enemy back. Nevertheless, the situation is hopeless. Yoshitomo sets fire to the palace, turning the battle into a melee, and the defenders are finally defeated.

Sutoku flees to Mount Nyoi, where he takes Buddhist vows, and then secludes himself at the temple of Ninna-ji. Yorinaga attempts to flee to Kitashirakawa but is killed on the way by a stray arrow. Tameyoshi and Tadamasa surrender, appealing to Yoshitomo and Kiyomori for mercy. Yoshitomo and Kiyomori refuse to forgive them their treason, and they are executed at Rokujōgawara.

**Chapter Three**: The execution of their leaders is only the beginning of the tragedy of the defeated warriors. All of Tameyoshi's many children are killed or executed, but most pathetic is the scene of the execution of his four young sons at Funaokayama. Overcome with grief, their mother throws herself into the Katsura River.

Due to Yorinaga's high rank, his surviving children are spared execution, and instead they are exiled to places far from the capital. Sutoku himself is exiled to Sanuki in Shikoku. For three years, he devotes himself to making a copy of the five Great Tendai Sutras (*Daijōkyō*), which he then sends to the capital as a sign of repentance. Go-Shirakawa is not appeased, however, and sends the offering back. Overcome with anger, Sutoku bites off his tongue and, with his own blood, writes a curse on Go-Shirakawa's line at the end of the scroll bearing the Great Tendai Sutras. He throws the scroll into the sea and dies in a state of deep mental torment.

Tametomo, the great archer of the battle at Shirakawa palace, is captured in Ōmi and taken back to the capital. After suffering the humiliation of having his shoulder muscles severed, he is exiled to the island of Ōshima off Izu. Far from defeated, however, he not only takes control of Ōshima but also establishes sway over the neighboring island of Onigashima. Shocked by the open defiance of this defeated enemy, the court dispatches a force of more than five hundred cavalry to attack him at Ōshima. After sinking the enemy ship with a huge arrow shot by his crippled arms, Tametomo commits *seppuku*, leaving behind one of the most illustrious names in the chronicles of great warriors.

This chapter. Kan'ei-era edition. Large ōhon book. Illustrations approximately 21.0 cm by 15.5 cm.

Chapter One. During the reign of Emperor Nijō, two of the favorites at court, Fuji-wara no Nobuyori and Shinzei Nyūdō (Fujiwara no Michinori), are on bad terms, and they exchange angry words on frequent occasions. This seething hostility finally erupts into open conflict when Shinzei exploits his influence with ex-Emperor Go-Shirakawa to block Nobuyori's appointment to the coveted position of commander of the imperial guards.

Playing on the fresh wounds of the Hōgen War, Nobuyori persuades Minamoto no Yoshitomo to join him in a plot against Go-Shirakawa, Shinzei, and Taira no Kiyomori, now the most powerful figure in the land. In the twelfth month of the first year of Heiji (1159), seizing the opportunity of Kiyomori's annual New Year pilgrimage to Kumano-dera, Yoshitomo stages a successful night attack on Go-Shirakawa's Sanjo palace and Shinzei's mansion. In the absence of Kiyomori, Nobuyori and Yoshitomo are soon in command of the capital.

# Heiji Monogatari

平治物語

## The Tale of Heiji

Three chapters. Kanei-era edition. Large upright book. Illustrations approximately 21.0 cm by 15.5 cm.

**Chapter One**: During the reign of Emperor Nijō, two of the favorites at court, Fujiwara no Nobuyori and Shinzei Nyūdō (Fujiwara no Michinori), are on bad terms, and they exchange angry words on frequent occasions. This seething hostility finally erupts into open conflict when Shinzei exploits his influence with ex-Emperor Go-Shirakawa to block Nobuyori's appointment to the coveted position of commander of the imperial guards.

Playing on the fresh wounds of the Hōgen War, Nobuyori persuades Minamoto no Yoshitomo to join him in a plot against Go-Shirakawa, Shinzei, and Taira no Kiyomori, now the most powerful figure in the land. In the twelfth month of the first year of Heiji (1159), seizing the opportunity of Kiyomori's annual New Year pilgrimage to Kumano-dera, Yoshitomo stages a successful night attack on Go-Shirakawa's Sanjō palace and Shinzei's mansion. In the absence of Kiyomori, Nobuyori and Yoshitomo are soon in command of the capital.

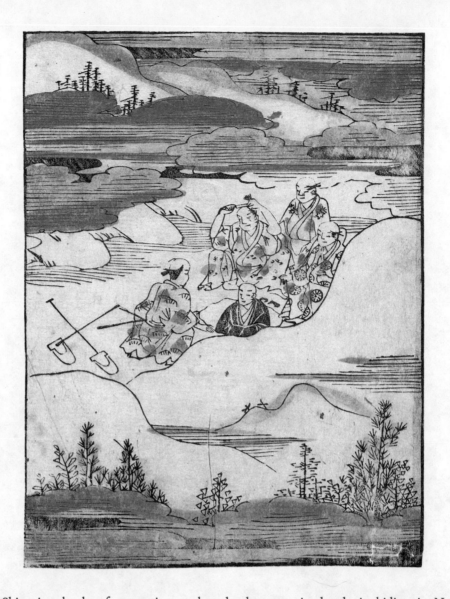

Shinzei, who has foreseen just such a development, is already in hiding in Nara. Yoshitomo's retainers quickly discover his hiding place, however, and after cruelly dispatching him they take his head back to the capital for public display. When Kiyomori receives the news that the capital has fallen to Nobuyori and Yoshitomo, he quickly returns from Kumano and successfully gathers his forces at his Rokuhara mansion. With Kiyomori's return, the Taira forces regain their confidence, and there is more cause for rejoicing when it is learned that Go-Shirakawa is departing for a splendid New Year's excursion to Ninna-ji and that Emperor Nijō himself plans to lead an excursion to Rokuhara, which will mean the addition of his personal retainers to the Taira force.

**Chapter Two**: Nobuyori and Yoshitomo have occupied the imperial palace, and Nobuyori is holding banquets there as if he were the emperor himself. It is here that the Taira, with a force now numbering over three thousand, stage their counterattack. Kiyomori's son Shigemori breaks through the Taiken Gate and fights his way to the inner garden of the emperor's chambers. Here he encounters Kamakura Akugenda Yoshihira, Yoshitomo's eldest son, and the two young men stage one of the most famous scenes of personal combat in all of Japanese literature. Akugenda is finally forced to retreat in

the face of a superior force, and withdraws in the direction of the Taira mansion at Rokuhara. In fact, however, this is all according to plan. Taira warriors fighting at the other gates draw out the Minamoto forces in a similar fashion, enabling their own larger force to slip past them. This force enters the palace and occupies it.

Left with no other choice, Yoshitomo attacks Rokuhara. Yoshihira fights as valiantly as before but is betrayed by one of his principal allies, Yorimasa, who switches sides to join the Taira. Confronted with insurmountable odds, Yoshitomo is forced to accept defeat. He flees the capital hoping to regroup his forces in the east. Nobuyori, who has already displayed his cowardice during the battles at the palace and Rokuhara, flees to Ninna-ji, where he begs Go-Shirakawa to grant him asylum. He is quickly captured, however, and taken back to Kyoto to be executed at Rokujōgawara.

At Ōhaka station in Mino, Yoshitomo is forced to kill his second son, Tomonaga, who has been severely wounded by the hostile monks of Mount Hiei during the flight from the capital. He proceeds to Utsumi in Owari to seek protection from Nagata no Shōji Tadamune, a trusted vassal. Tadamune, himself a Taira, has his own fears and ambitions. Feigning loyalty, he offers his protection and invites Yoshitomo to his own quarters.

the face of a superior force, and withdraws in the direction of the Taira mansion at Rokuhara. In fact, however, this is all according to plan. Taira warriors fighting at the other gates draw out the Minamoto forces in a similar fashion, enabling their own larger force to slip past them. This force enters the palace and occupies it.

Left with no other choice, Yoshitomo attacks Rokuhara. Yoshihira fights as valiantly as before but is betrayed by one of his principal allies, Yorimasa, who switches sides to join the Taira. Confronted with insurmountable odds, Yoshitomo is forced to accept defeat. He flees the capital hoping to regroup his forces in the east. Nobuyori, who has already displayed his cowardice during the battles at the palace and Rokuhara, flees to Ninna-ji, where he begs Go-Shirakawa to grant him asylum. He is quickly captured, however, and taken back to Kyoto to be executed at Rokujōgawara.

At Aohaka Station in Mino, Yoshitomo is forced to kill his second son Tomonaga, who has been severely wounded by the hostile monks of Mount Hiei during the flight from the capital. He proceeds to Utsumi in Owari to seek protection from Nagata no Shōji Tadamune, a trusted vassal. Tadamune, himself a Taira, has his own fears and ambitions. Feigning loyalty, he offers his protection and invites Yoshitomo to his own quarters.

Without suspecting treachery, Yoshitomo accepts the offer of a hot bath, but once defenseless he is cruelly murdered.

**Chapter Three**: Akugenda Yoshihira, who has been in hiding at Ishiyama-dera in Ōmi, is captured and killed. Yoshitomo's third son, Yoritomo, is captured at Sekigahara and taken back to the capital. Like all of Yoshitomo's children, he is under sentence of death, but Ike no Zenni, the widow of Taira no Tadamori, Kiyomori's famous father, intercedes on his behalf and his life is spared. He is exiled to Izu where he again meets Ike no Zenni.

Tokiwa, Yoshitomo's beloved consort, is in hiding in Uda with their three youngest sons. Kiyomori seizes her mother as a hostage, and Tokiwa is forced to appear with the children before Kiyomori. Overcome by her great beauty and refinement, he spares her and her children.

The youngest, Ushiwaka, is sent to Kurama-dera to become a priest, but he soon develops an interest in martial skills. Ushiwaka encounters Kichiji, a gold merchant from the north, who tells him stories of the powerful Fujiwara of the province of Ōshū. Dreaming of an alliance between the Minamoto and the Ōshū Fujiwara, Ushiwaka sets out with Kichiji. Along the way, at Kagami Station, Ushiwaka goes through his capping ceremony and gives himself the name Yoshitsune. Finally, he arrives in Ōshū, where he receives the protection of Fujiwara no Hidehira.

After twenty-one years in exile, Yoritomo is encouraged by a priest called Mongaku Shōnin to raise an army. Upon hearing this news, Yoshitsune rushes to join his elder brother. In the subsequent Genpei War, he displays his military genius in a series of brilliant campaigns that lead to the total defeat of the Taira. Unfortunately, he has aroused Yoritomo's jealousy and suspicion, and he is eventually forced to seek protection once again from Hidehira in Ōshū. Hidehira dies soon afterward, and Yoshitsune is betrayed and killed by Hidehira's son Yasuhira. Yoritomo accomplishes the redoubtable feat of defeating the Ōshū Fujiwara and unifies the country under his Kamakura shogunate.

# *Gikeiki* 義 経 記

## The Chronicle of Yoshitsune

Eight chapters. Kanei-era edition. Large upright book. Eight volumes extant. Volume four of the set in the author's collection is from a different edition (p. 59) entitled *Hōgan Monogatari* (The Tale of Hōgan Yoshitsune). Illustrations approximately 20.0 cm by 16.0 cm. (For a complete translation of *Gikeiki*, see Helen Craig McCullough, *Yoshitsune: A Fifteenth Century Japanese Chronicle* [Stanford, Calif.: Stanford University Press, 1966].)

Gikeiki *takes up the story where* Heiji Monogatari *ends (or, as in the case of the* ko-katsujibon tanrokubon *editions, the two stories overlap).*

**Chapter One**: After Yoshitomo's defeat in the Heiji War and his flight from the capital, his children are either killed or forced to languish in hiding. Tokiwa, his beloved consort, is made to bring Ushiwaka and his two elder brothers to Rokuhara. Just as Taira no Kiyomori is deciding whether to torture the children by fire or by water, he is struck by the sight of Tokiwa and is persuaded to spare the children in exchange for her favors. Ushiwaka is sent to Yamashina, where he remains until his sixth year.

54

In the second month of Ushiwaka's sixth year, Tokiwa, fearful that rumors of his precocity will reach Kiyomori, appeals to Tōkōbō, the abbot of Kurama-dera, to accept Ushiwaka as his disciple. Ushiwaka is admitted to Kurama-dera as a temple page and is given the name Shanaō. At first Shanaō devotes himself entirely to his studies, reciting sutras and poring over the Chinese classics night and day, but after an encounter with the priest Shōmon, the grandson of Yoshitomo's wet nurse, he forgets his devotions completely and thinks of nothing but rebellion. Soon he is taking every opportunity to slip away to the Kibune Shrine in the valley of Sōjō no Tani near Kurama-dera to practice martial arts. Finally, in his fifteenth year, he meets the Ōshū gold merchant Kichiji Nobutaka, who tells him of Fujiwara no Hidehira, scion of the illustrious Ōshū Fujiwara family, which throughout Japan's history has never bowed to central authority. Shanaō resolves to accompany Kichiji to Ōshū to seek an alliance with Hidehira.

**Chapter Two**: On the way to Ōshū, Shanaō has a fantastic duel with a band of ferocious robbers at Kagami Station. He has his capping ceremony performed by the chief priest of Atsuta Shrine, who is Yoshitomo's father-in-law, Fujiwara no Suenori, and gives himself the name Sama no Kurō Yoshitsune. At a place called Itahana in Kōzuke, he meets Ise no Saburō Yoshimori, who is to become one of his most trusted retainers. After these and many other adventures, Yoshitsune finally reaches Hidehira's splendid capital, Hiraizumi. Hidehira agrees to an alliance, and, after spending some time in Hiraizumi, Yoshitsune returns to the capital to pursue his studies and keep an eye on the Taira. There he hears of a magical sixteen-volume book on the art of war, *Liutao*, which is in the possession of a ying-yang master called Kiichi Hōgen. Kiichi attempts to have him killed, but Yoshitsune defeats his assassins and escapes with the book. Not only has Kiichi lost his magical book, but also his youngest and favorite daughter, who has fallen in love with Yoshitsune, is brokenhearted when Yoshitsune makes his escape and leaves her.

**Chapter Three**: During the period in Yoshitsune's life covered in the first two chapters, Oniwaka, the son of Benshō, abbot of all the temples and shrines on Mount Kumano, is sent to Mount Hiei. He is shunned by the other priests, however, because of his ugliness and his violent behavior. After burning the temple buildings at Mount Shosha, he commits the sacrilege of shaving his own head and gives himself the name Musashibō Benkei. Thereupon, he leaves Mount Hiei for the capital, where he embarks on a plan to steal one thousand swords from passers-by. He encounters Yoshitsune at Kiyomizu-dera and they fight one of the most famous duels in Japanese literature. Yoshitsune roundly defeats Benkei, and Benkei swears an oath of fealty to him, becoming Yoshitsune's most stalwart retainer.

The two of them depart for Ōshū to escape the Taira. In the fourth year of Jishō (1180) Yoritomo raises his battle flag with a night assault upon Izumi Hangan Kanetaka, a vassal of the Taira. This marks the beginning of the Genpei War, chronicled in *Heike Monogatari*. Yoshitsune gathers his small band of allies and rushes to join his elder brother.

Chapter Four: Yoshitsune meets his elder brother, Minamoto no Yoritomo, for the first time at Ukishimagahara. He is made the commanding general of the Minamoto forces and, in the third year of Juei (1185), marches on the capital to drive out the Taira. Later, at the battles of Ichinotani and Dannoura, he annihilates the Taira. He attempts to enter Kamakura with the enemy commander, Taira no Munemori, Munemori's son, and thirty other prisoners. Kajiwara no Kagetoki, Yoritomo's principal adviser, playing on his master's jealousy of Yoshitsune's military prowess, convinces him that Yoshitsune is disloyal, and Yoritomo orders Yoshitsune to wait at Koshigoe. In despair, Yoshitsune returns to the capital. He is driven out of the capital as well and, failing in an attempt to flee to Shikoku, is finally forced to go into hiding in the Yoshino mountains.

Chapter Five: In constant danger, Yoshitsune resolves to send his beloved mistress, Shizuka, back to the capital. She is robbed and deserted by her escorts but finally manages to find her way to the Zaō Gongen temple. Her identity is revealed when she dances, for she is the most famous shirabyoshi dancer in the land. She is seized by the monks of the temple, forced to divulge the whereabouts of Yoshitsune's hiding place, and sent to the capital. The monks attack Yoshitsune, and after a desperately fought battle, Yoshitsune's force is scattered pell-mell. Satō no Tadanobu, one of Yoshitsune's commanders, stays behind to hold off the enemy. He stages a superhuman performance in battle with the monks and then eludes them in a series of clever and sometimes magical maneuvers.

Chapter Six: Tadanobu escapes to the capital and begins his search for Yoshitsune but is betrayed by his lover. Assassins are sent from Rokuhara. Even in his last hour, Tadanobu succeeds in frustrating his enemies by killing himself.

Shizuka, who is with child, is discovered by Yoritomo's retainers at Hōshōji and taken to Kamakura, where her newly born son is killed. Shortly afterward, she is forced to perform a shirabyoshi for Yoritomo at the Lower Hachiman Shrine.

**Chapter Four**: Yoshitsune meets his elder brother, Minamoto no Yoritomo, for the first time at Ukishimagahara. He is made the commanding general of the Minamoto forces and, in the third year of Juei (1184), marches on the capital to drive out the Taira. Later, at the battles of Ichinotani and Dannoura, he annihilates the Taira. He attempts to enter Kamakura with the enemy commander, Taira no Munemori, Munemori's son, and thirty other prisoners. Kajiwara no Kagetoki, Yoritomo's principal adviser, playing on his master's jealousy of Yoshitsune's military prowess, convinces him that Yoshitsune is disloyal, and Yoritomo orders Yoshitsune to wait at Koshigoe. In despair, Yoshitsune returns to the capital. He is driven out of the capital as well and, failing in an attempt to flee to Shikoku, is finally forced to go into hiding in the Yoshino mountains.

**Chapter Five**: In constant danger, Yoshitsune resolves to send his beloved mistress, Shizuka, back to the capital. She is robbed and deserted by her escorts but finally manages to find her way to the Zaō Gongen temple. Her identity is revealed when she dances, for she is the most famous *shirabyōshi* dancer in the land. She is seized by the monks of the temple, forced to divulge the whereabouts of Yoshitsune's hiding place, and sent to the capital. The monks attack Yoshitsune, and after a desperately fought battle Yoshitsune's force is scattered pell-mell. Satō no Tadanobu, one of Yoshitsune's commanders stays behind to hold off the enemy. He stages a superhuman performance in battle with the monks and then eludes them in a series of clever and sometimes magical maneuvers.

**Chapter Six**: Tadanobu escapes to the capital and begins his search for Yoshitsune but is betrayed by his lover. Assassins are sent from Rokuhara. Even in his last hour, Tadanobu succeeds in frustrating his enemies by killing himself.

Shizuka, who is with child, is discovered by Yoritomo's retainers at Hosshō-ji and taken to Kamakura, where her newly born son is killed. Shortly afterward, she is forced to perform a *shirabyōshi* for Yoritomo at the Lower Hachiman Shrine.

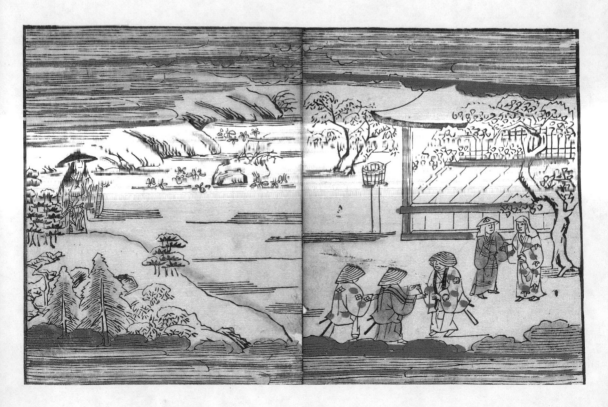

 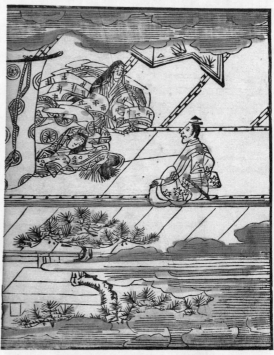

**Chapter Seven**: In the second year of Bunji (1186) Yoshitsune gathers sixteen scattered retainers and sets off to seek refuge in Ōshū. Evading or fighting off countless enemies along the way, they finally make their way to Hidehira's castle at Hiraizumi.

**Chapter Eight**: In the twelfth month of the fourth year of Bunji (1188), Hidehira dies, leaving a will enjoining his sons to uphold his pledge of loyalty to Yoshitsune. One of his sons, Yasuhira, ignores his father's dying request and, in the fourth month of the fifth year of Bunji, attacks Yoshitsune at Takadachi. Benkei and Yoshitsune's other retainers fight valiantly against overwhelming odds but are finally defeated. Kanefusa, one of Yoshitsune's loyal retainers, holds off the advancing enemy while Yoshitsune commits *seppuku* and then, in tears, kills his master's wife and two children.

# Soga Monogatari　　　　　　　　　　曽 我 物 語

## The Tale of the Soga

Twelve chapters. Kanei-era edition. Large upright book. Twelve volumes. Illustrations approximately 21.0 cm by 14.5 cm.

**Chapter One**: Kudō no Saemon Suketsune lodges a suit with Kiyomori's government in Kyoto against his uncle, Itō no Jirō Sukechika, in a dispute over the lands in their respective domains. Defeated in court, he vents his anger by ordering two of his retainers to murder Sukechika's son, Kawazu no Saburō Sukeshige, whom they duly slay. Concerned for the safety of Sukeshige's two young sons, four-year-old Ichiman and two-year-old Hakoō, Sukechika arranges for his son's widow to marry Soga no Tarō Sukenobu.

**Chapter Two**: Minamoto no Yoritomo, who has been exiled to Izu, becomes intimate with Sukechika's daughter, and she bears him a son. Fearing the wrath of the Taira, Sukechika has the child killed. In the eighth month of the fourth year of Jishō (1180), Yoritomo rebels against the Taira and emerges victorious from the subsequent Genpei War, bringing the entire country under the dominion of his new government in Kamakura. Sukechika is executed for having murdered Yoritomo's son and opposed the Minamoto during the Genpei War.

**Chapter Three**: Even as young children, Ichiman and Hakoō are constant in their burning desire to take revenge on Suketsune for the murder of their father. Suketsune has not forgotten them either, and he reminds Yoritomo that Sukechika's grandchildren are still alive. Moreover, he slanders them, suggesting that, young as they are, they are already planning rebellion. Yoritomo orders Sukenobu to bring the boys to Kamakura. He commands that they be executed at Yuigahama, but he is opposed by most of his vassals and is finally forced to spare them.

**Chapter Four**: Ichiman's capping ceremony is performed and he is given the name Soga no Jūrō Sukenari. Hakoō is sent to Hakone to enter the priesthood. However, he has no intention of becoming a priest and, after consulting his elder brother, leaves Hakone. He persuades Hōjō Tokimasa, one of Yoritomo's leading vassals, to perform his capping ceremony and is given the name Soga no Gorō Tokimune. His mother is greatly angered by this and disinherits him. In the meantime, Jūrō has become intimate with a courtesan named Ōiso no Tora, and he continues his relationship with her for the remaining three years of his life.

**Chapter Five**: A great lover of the hunt, Yoritomo embarks on hunting expeditions to famous gaming spots in various parts of the country: to Asama, Miharano, Nasuno, and Asazuma. Hearing of these expeditions, the Soga brothers follow Yoritomo, hoping

for a chance to attack Suketsune. On every occasion, however, their plans are frustrated by chance, or because Suketsune is too well guarded.

**Chapter Six**: Hearing that Yoritomo is planning an expedition to the plain at the foot of Mount Fuji, the brothers vow that this time they will carry out their revenge, even at the cost of their own lives. Jūrō goes to Ōiso to bid farewell to Tora. In the meantime, however, Wada no Yoshimori, one of Yoritomo's vassals, has taken up lodgings in the same inn with one hundred and eighty of his retainers. Jūrō is invited to Yoshimori's banquet in the evening, and Tora is forced to attend them. Yoshimori makes her choose between them by holding out her *sake* cup to the man of her choice. When she chooses Jūrō, there is danger of a serious quarrel, but Gorō suddenly arrives to save the situation. He challenges Yoshimori's son, Asahina no Saburō Yoshihide, to a test of strength, and his display of prowess and martial skill so frightens Yoshimori that the latter represses his belligerent jealousy.

**Chapter Seven**: Gorō appeals to Jūrō to intercede with their mother on his behalf. They visit their mother, and Jūrō persuades her to forgive his younger brother. Now with no regrets left in the world, the two brothers set off to find Yoritomo's procession.

**Chapters Eight, Nine, and Ten**: On their way to Mount Fuji, the brothers stop off at the temple in Hakone. As a parting gift to his erstwhile disciple, the abbot presents Gorō with a pair of famous swords. Upon arriving at Yoritomo's camp on the plain beneath Mount Fuji, the brothers carefully scout the encampments of the various great lords, finally resolving to carry out their plan that very night. They write a farewell letter to their mother and send two of their men back to Soga with it. They are successful in penetrating Suketsune's encampment, and they kill him in his bedclothes. They are quickly surrounded by his retainers, and, after a brilliant defense against overwhelming odds, Jūrō is killed and Gorō is captured and then executed.

**Chapters Eleven and Twelve**: Hearing of Jūrō's death, Ōiso no Tora becomes a nun. Subsequently she travels to Soga to meet the brothers' mother and accompanies her to Hakone, where they intend to devote themselves to devotions on behalf of the brothers' tormented souls. Later, Tora becomes a wandering nun and travels all over the country doing devotions before finally returning to Ōiso, where she retires to a grass hut in the grounds of a temple called Kōrai-ji.

74

# *Kōwakamai* Librettos
## (*Kōwaka Bukyoku*)

## 幸若舞曲

# Fushimi Tokiwa 伏見常盤

## Tokiwa's Flight to Fushimi

Kanei-era edition. Large upright book. One volume (incomplete). Four illustrations, approximately 19.0 cm by 14.0 cm. Color plates include illustrations from another edition entitled *Fushimi* (illustrations approximately 19.0 cm by 13.0 cm).

*The plot of this* kōwakamai *libretto is an elaboration of the story of Lady Tokiwa's desperate flight from the capital after Yoshitomo's defeat, which is briefly related in the final chapter of* Heiji Monogatari.

Tokiwa Gozen, whose father was Umezu Genzaemon and whose mother was Katsura no Saishō, enters the service of Kujō-in, the consort of ex-Emperor Konoe, and is given the name Totsuko no Mae. One day, when Totsuko is still quite young, it is decided that there will be a contest among all the women in Kujō-in's service. Out of a thousand

beautiful women, Totsuko is chosen, along with Ayame and Makomo. Ayame and Makomo are fond of making themselves up with gorgeous cosmetics and changing clothes at the slightest whim. Though she never wears makeup and is more modest in her attire, Totsuko always manages to preserve her quiet beauty. So impressed is Kujō-in with this charming little girl that she gives her a new name, Tokiwa, which means evergreen, an allusion to her constant beauty.

Minamoto no Yoshitomo catches a glimpse of Tokiwa and resolves to make her his own. He repeatedly presses the emperor for permission to approach her but is sent away disappointed every time. He finally wins permission to marry Tokiwa in reward for his valor in putting down an assault on the Shishinden, the emperor's personal compound. She is sixteen, and he is thirty. Tokiwa bears him three sons, Imawaka, Otowaka, and Ushiwaka.

In the first year of Heiji (1159), Yoshitomo is defeated in the Heiji War and killed in tragic circumstances by a stray arrow as he attempts to flee to his stronghold in the east. On the seventeenth day of the first month of Eiryaku (1160), Tokiwa slips stealthily out of Yoshitomo's mansion in Kyoto, leading Imawaka and Otowaka by the hand and clutching the infant Ushiwaka to her breast. She stops at Kiyomizu-dera on the outskirts of the capital to pray to Kannon, the goddess of mercy, for the future of her young sons and then leaves the capital for the province of Yamato to seek refuge there.

On foot with three young children complaining in tearful voices of the bitter cold, the snow, and the blast of the winter wind, she can make it no further than Mount Kohata by nightfall. In a valley, she sees the faint glimmer of a light, and finally makes her way to the door of a poor house that appears to belong to a commoner. She begs for shelter for herself and her children, but the old man who peeks out from the door quickly shuts it, suspecting that she must be one of the Minamoto fleeing the capital in the aftermath of the war. With no place to turn, Tokiwa brushes away the snow below the eaves of the house and, removing her outer kimino, spreads it on the ground for the boys to lie down on. With a broad merchant woman's hat held against the wind and the snow, she quietly begins to invoke the name of the Buddha Amida.

Struck by her pathetic plight, the old man and his wife take pity on her and allow Tokiwa and her children inside the house. Her almost supernatural beauty and her elegant responses in an exchange of poems quickly betray her high rank, and, deeply impressed, the old couple offer to conceal her and her three sons in a Buddhist sanctuary on their land.

After several days in hiding, they are discovered by five young women from nearby houses, who bring crude country wine and beg to hear Tokiwa's story. Disguising her true identity, Tokiwa tells them that her husband is having an affair with a woman of dubious repute so she has resolved to return with her children to her father's home in Uda. The old man suggests that the girls sing songs from their native lands to comfort Tokiwa. Each of the girls is from a different part of Japan: from Izumo, Harima, Tango, Izumi, and Ōmi. This is the climax of the dance. One after the other, they stand and perform the dances of their childhood homes, accompanying themselves with songs. The scene becomes lively as the dancers grow more and more spirited, wishing Tokiwa good fortune at the end of her long journey.

# Fue no Maki 笛 の 巻

## The Story of the Flute Book

Kanei-era edition. Large upright book. One volume. Illustrations approximately 19.7 cm by 13.5 cm. *This kōwakamai libretto relates one of the legends concerning Yoshitsune's years as a temple page at Kurama-dera. This episode does not appear in the first chapter of* Gikeiki.

As a young boy, Yoshitsune is sent to Kurama-dera to become the disciple of Tōkōbō. For a time, he devotes himself diligently to study, poring over the classics and mastering the most difficult calligraphic styles. Concerned that he should have something with which to amuse himself, his mother, Tokiwa Gozen, is struck by the thought that there would be nothing better for such a sophisticated child than classical music and that, of all the instruments of court music, there is none so elegant as the flute. She obtains a flute from the musician Mitajirō of Yodonotsu and sends it to Yoshitsune at Kurama-dera.

Yoshitsune is delighted and, before the year is out, masters one hundred and twenty songs from the repertoire of court music. Aware of the wonderful qualities of the flute he has received from Tokiwa, he concludes that it is useless to own a treasure if one knows nothing of its background. He invites Mitajirō to Kurama-dera and begs him to reveal the flute's history. Mitajirō is delighted, and tells him the following story.

Long, long ago, Kōbō Daishi traveled to China, where he visited Jiangsu-si and mastered the secrets of Shingon Buddhism. Later he traveled to India to worship Manjusri at Grdhrakuta. On the way back to China, he passed the waterfall of Mount Congling, where his eye was caught by three stalks of bamboo growing near the cascading water. Drawing his sword, he cut them, and, thinking whimsically that if it were so ordained he might see them again in Japan, threw them into the Liusha River.

After returning to Japan, Kōbō Daishi traveled to his native land of Byōbu-ura in Sanuki to visit his parents' graves. As he was walking along the beach at Byōbu-ura, he happened to notice three stalks of bamboo floating in the surf. He bent down to pick them out of the water and, at that moment, realized that they were the same three stalks of bamboo that he had thrown into the Liusha River in Central Asia. Thinking this karmic relation strange indeed, he took them back to the capital and had them made into three flutes, which he named Ōsuiryō, Kosuiryō, and Aoba. The flute called Aoba (green leaf) was so named because, despite the fact that the bamboo itself had faded during the long sea journey, there was a single green leaf growing from one of its joints.

Afterward, the three flutes were kept in the emperor's private compound and were considered to be national treasures. During a flower-viewing excursion to Yoshino, however, the flute called Aoba was given to the famous Middle Captain Sagoromo, whose rendition of a song called "Manjūraku" was said to have so delighted souls lost in purgatory that they were rescued from their suffering and, laughing and dancing, became Bodhisattvas. This same Middle Captain lived in Yodonotsu, and, on a certain occasion, he gave the flute to a musician called Mitatarō, Mitajirō's grandfather. Mitajirō had received the flute from his grandfather and, at Tokiwa's request, had given it to Yoshitsune as a gift.

At the completion of his story, Mitajirō assures Yoshitsune that, as long as he has this flute, he will be protected from danger by all the Buddhas and Shintō gods. He warns

Yoshitsune to keep it by his side. Yoshitsune claps his hands in delight at the story and makes Mitajirō repeat it three times while he records it in a book. He calls the book *Fue no Maki* (The Flute Book). It is said that this book still survives in the storehouse of Kurama-dera.

鞍馬寺

83

童子

85

Kan'ei-era edition. Large upright book. Two volumes. Sixteen illustrations, approximately 18.5 cm by 14.5 cm.

In the first year of Kenkyū (1190), Minamoto no Yoritomo arranges an excursion to the capital in order to present a grant of land to Tōdai-ji in Nara. Akushichibyōe Kagekiyo, one of the last survivors of the once-mighty Taira family, plans to seize this opportunity to take revenge on Yoritomo. He disguises himself as a priest and manages to get past the guards at the temple's Tegai Gate, but he is recognized by Hatakeyama no Shigetada, Yoritomo's bodyguard.

# Kagekiyo 景清
## Taira no Kagekiyo

Kanei-era edition. Large upright book. Two volumes. Sixteen illustrations, approximately 18.5 cm by 14.5 cm.

In the first year of Kenkyū (1190), Minamoto no Yoritomo arranges an excursion to the capital in order to present a grant of land to Tōdai-ji in Nara. Akushichibyōe Kagekiyo, one of the last survivors of the once mighty Taira family, plans to seize this opportunity to take revenge on Yoritomo. He disguises himself as a priest and manages to get past the guards at the temple's Tegai Gate, but he is recognized by Hatakeyama no Shigetada, Yoritomo's bodyguard.

On the following day, he disguises himself as a mountain priest and waits for a chance to approach Yoritomo at the temple of Hannya-ji. Again, he is recognized by Shigetada, and is forced to flee to Kyoto. He hears that Yoritomo is planning a visit to Kiyomizu-dera. This time, he daubs himself with lacquer in order to hide his identity and mingles with the beggars in the temple courtyard. Once again, however, his disguise is penetrated by Shigetada. Things continue in this fashion until Kagekiyo has attempted to assassinate Yoritomo thirty-seven times, each attempt ending in failure. Kagekiyo leaves the capital to seek refuge in Owari, where his father-in-law is the chief priest of the Atsuta Shrine.

Made uneasy by Kagekiyo's repeated attempts on his life, Yoritomo has notices posted throughout the capital offering a reward for information regarding Kagekiyo's whereabouts. Kagekiyo has long been intimate with a courtesan called Akoō, who lives on Kiyomizu hill, and she has borne him two sons. Tempted by the offer of a reward, however, Akoō requests an audience with Yoritomo at Rokuhara and suggests a plan for capturing Kagekiyo. Yoritomo agrees to the plan.

Akoō lures Kagekiyo to Kiyomizu-dera for a moon-viewing excursion and, after pressing cup after cup of *sake* on him, leads a force from Rokuhara to his hiding place. Enraged by Akoō's betrayal, Kagekiyo kills their two sons and, after slaughtering his pursuers, makes his escape to Owari.

Seeking revenge for the murder of her sons, Akoō offers to betray Kagekiyo's hiding place again, but by now Yoritomo has become disgusted with her and, after putting her on display in the capital as an unfaithful wife, has her bound and thrown into the sea at Inasegafuchi.

On Kajiwara no Kagetoki's advice, Yoritomo has Kagekiyo's father-in-law arrested and imprisoned, forcing Kagekiyo to come forward in order to save the old man's life. Kagekiyo is imprisoned at Rokuhara. He represses his anger for some time, but finally, enraged by comments ridiculing him for allowing himself to be captured alive, he makes a violent escape and flees to Kiyomizu-dera. There he entreats Kannon to aid him in his quest for revenge. Slowly he returns to his senses and, realizing that his father-in-law is still in danger, goes back to the prison.

Yoritomo orders that Kagekiyo be executed at Rokujōgawara, and Kagekiyo is beheaded. Upon his return to Rokuhara, however, Yoritomo is shocked to discover that another Kagekiyo has appeared in the Rokuhara prison and is behaving as if nothing at all has happened. Slowly, it dawns on Yoritomo that the Kiyomizu-dera Kannon must have taken Kagekiyo's place at Rokujōgawara. Awed by this divine intervention, he orders Kagekiyo's release. Kagekiyo is deeply grateful, but he declares that, nevertheless, he is unable to repress his obsession with revenge whenever he looks upon Yoritomo. He begs to have his eyes gouged out and to be allowed to leave the capital for Tsukushi (Kyushu). Yoritomo assents to this and grants him the domain of Miyazaki in the province of Hyūga.

Before leaving for Tsukushi, Kagekiyo visits Kiyomizu-dera to thank Kannon. Miraculously, he finds that he is suddenly able to see from his empty eye sockets. He becomes a fervent devotee of Kannon, and when he finally arrives in Kyushu he has a temple constructed in Miyazaki. He gives this temple the name Shin Kiyomizu-dera (New Kiyomizu Temple) and is unfailing in his daily devotions until his death at the advanced age of eighty-two.

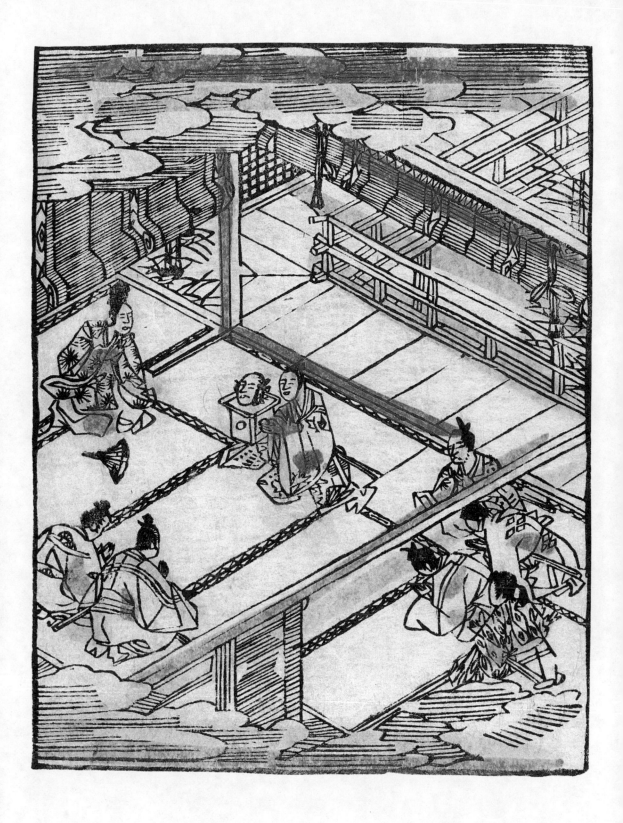

Kanei-era edition. Large upright book. One volume. Six illustrations; approximately 18.5 cm by 18.5 cm

*This story is an elaboration of an episode in chapter seven of Gikeiki.*

In the first month of the second year of Bunji (1186), Yoshitsune is still in hiding near the capital in constant danger of being discovered by Yoritomo's retainers. He resolves to flee the capital and seek refuge in Oshu, where Fujiwara no Hidehira had sheltered him in his youth. He sets off accompanied by his wife, Benkei, and eleven other retainers, all disguised as wandering ascetics. After many narrow escapes, they reach Togashi in the province of Kaga. They are detained there by Togashi no Suke, one of Yoritomo's minor vassals, who suspects their true identity. In his usual fashion, Benkei persuades Togashi no Suke that they are indeed wandering ascetics from Haguro, on a pilgrimage to collect offerings for Todai-ji in Nara. As proof of this, he confidently intones a register of gifts, all of which he extemporizes in a show of great dramatic verve. Togashi no Suke is completely won over. He invites them to his mansion, where he lavishes them with gifts. Finally, they are free to continue their journey.

They are stopped once again at the Nyoi River crossing, but Benkei displays his brilliant wit once again, this time by flogging Yoshitsune, who is disguised as a temple page, an inconceivable act if this were in fact his lord, Yoshitsune. They are allowed to cross the river, and from there make their way to Noto, Etchu, and finally to Naoenotsu, the capital of Echigo. They seek lodgings at the mansion of Naoe no Taro, whose elder brother, Naoe no Jiro, is indebted to Yoshiie, Yoshitsune's famous ancestor. The fishermen at the harbor and Naoe no Taro's retainers suspect that the party is, in fact, made up of Yoshitsune and his retainers. Led by Naoe no Taro, they arm themselves with bows and arrows, and Yoshitsune's quarters are surrounded by a mob of seven or eight hundred people.

Yoshitsune is warned by one of the women of the house, and, after ordering his wife and his retainers to hide themselves, he goes out to confront the mob. For a time, he is successful in tricking them, saying, "If I were indeed Sama Karo Yoshitsune, would I be traveling with such a small force." However, Naoe no Taro is not so easily fooled, and insists that this temple page indeed bears a close resemblance to Yoshitsune. After several more exchanges, the mob begins to demand loudly that the party's baggage be searched. Yoshitsune has no choice but to submit to the search.

The first few panniers do indeed contain Buddhist images and ceremonial objects, but in the remaining baskets are found suits of mail, wigs, gorgeous sashes, Chinese mirrors, and weapons. Yoshitsune attempts to explain these objects away as Benkei had done at Togashi, but the mob is unconvinced, and it is decided that one of the party should be taken to Kamakura for investigation. At a loss, Yoshitsune raises his conch shell to his mouth and blows a mighty blast, signaling to Benkei and his other retainers to make their appearance. In his usual fashion, Benkei calms the mob and, indeed, manages to terrify them with the calamities that would befall them as a result of desecrating holy

# Oisagashi 笈さがし

## The Baggage Search at Naoenotsu

Kanei-era edition. Large upright book. One volume. Six illustrations, approximately 18.5 cm by 13.5 cm.

*This story is an elaboration of an episode in chapter seven of* Gikeiki.

In the first month of the second year of Bunji (1186), Yoshitsune is still in hiding near the capital, in constant danger of being discovered by Yoritomo's retainers. He resolves to flee the capital and seek refuge in Ōshū, where Fujiwara no Hidehira had sheltered him in his youth. He sets off accompanied by his wife, Benkei, and eleven other retainers, all disguised as wandering ascetics. After many narrow escapes, they reach Togashi in the province of Kaga. They are detained there by Togashi no Suke, one of Yoritomo's minor vassals, who suspects their true identity. In his usual fashion, Benkei persuades Togashi no Suke that they are indeed wandering ascetics from Haguro, on a pilgrimage to collect offerings for Tōdai-ji in Nara. As proof of this, he confidently intones a register of gifts, all of which he extemporizes in a show of great dramatic verve. Togashi no Suke is completely won over. He invites them to his mansion, where he lavishes them with gifts. Finally they are free to continue their journey.

They are stopped once again at the Nyoi River crossing, but Benkei displays his brilliant wit once again, this time by flogging Yoshitsune, who is disguised as a temple page, an inconceivable act if this were in fact his lord, Yoshitsune. They are allowed to cross the river, and from there make their way to Nōtō, Etchū, and finally to Naoenotsu, the capital of Echigo. They seek lodgings at the mansion of Naoe no Tarō, whose elder brother, Naoe no Jirō, is indebted to Yoshiie, Yoshitsune's famous ancestor. The fishermen at the harbor and Naoe no Tarō's retainers suspect that the party is, in fact, made up of Yoshitsune and his retainers. Led by Naoe no Tarō, they arm themselves with bows and arrows, and Yoshitsune's quarters are surrounded by a mob of seven or eight hundred people.

Yoshitsune is warned by one of the women of the house, and, after ordering his wife and his retainers to hide themselves, he goes out to confront the mob. For a time, he is successful in tricking them, saying, "If I were indeed Sama Kurō Yoshitsune, would I be traveling with such a small force?" However, Naoe no Tarō is not so easily fooled, and insists that this temple page indeed bears a close resemblance to Yoshitsune. After several more exchanges, the mob begins to demand loudly that the party's baggage be searched. Yoshitsune has no choice but to submit to the search.

The first five panniers do indeed contain Buddhist images and ceremonial objects, but in the remaining baskets are found suits of mail, wigs, gorgeous sashes, Chinese mirrors, and weapons. Yoshitsune attempts to explain these objects away as Benkei had done at Togashi, but the mob is unconvinced, and it is decided that one of the party should be taken to Kamakura for investigation. At a loss, Yoshitsune raises his conch shell to his mouth and blows a mighty blast, signaling to Benkei and his other retainers to make their appearance. In his usual fashion, Benkei calms the mob and, indeed, manages to terrify them with the calamities that would befall them as a result of desecrating holy

93

objects. He recovers their baggage and forces Naoe no Tarō to extend their stay at his mansion.

Anxious to be on their way, they exchange a precious sword in a beautiful white hand-bound scabbard for one of Naoe no Tarō's boats, a vessel called *Kotaka* (*Little Hawk*). They set off from Naoenotsu harbor with a gentle wind in their sails, Yoshitsune's retainers rowing hardily. Suddenly, however, lightning flashes from the peak of Mount Hoku on Sado Island, a peal of thunder roars through the sky, and a great wind begins to toss their tiny ship. Benkei and Ise no Saburō Yoshimori, another of Yoshitsune's stalwart retainers, run back and forth from prow to stern working desperately to keep the vessel afloat. Suddenly, out of nowhere, a huge fleet of ships appears, flying the red flag of the Taira. On board are the spirits of the Taira killed in battle at Ichinotani, Yashima, and Dannoura.

Benkei slings a linen ascetic's robe over his armor and, donning his helmet, leaps to the ship's prow. Filling his mighty lungs, he intones a chant for wandering souls. The mysterious nuances of his booming voice travel unwaveringly across the water, and, placated, the ghosts of the Taira disappear beneath the waves. In the same instant, the wind dies down, the sky clears, and the sea becomes calm.

# Izumigajō 和泉が城

## The Battle at Izumi Castle

Kanei-era edition. Large upright book. One volume. Nine illustrations extant. Illustrations approximately 18.6 cm by 14.0 cm. (Note: color plates were made from a copy of this edition in the collection of the late Yoshida Shigeru.)

*Although this episode is not mentioned in the last chapter of* Gikeiki, *it is clearly based on a legend elaborating the betrayal of Yoshitsune by Hidehira's sons.*

Yoshitsune reaches Hiraizumi, Hidehira's capital in Ōshū, late in the second year of Bunji (1186). He receives a splendid welcome from Hidehira, who orders that a great castle be built for him on the banks of the Koromo River, near his own castle. Yoshitsune calls his new fortress Takadachi and, with the vast resources of the Ōshū Fujiwara at his disposal, begins to assemble a large force.

97

In Kamakura, Yoshitsune's old enemy, Kajiwara no Kagetoki, hears rumors of his activities and summons the abbot of the Lower Hachiman Shrine. He orders the abbot to perform services invoking the gods to put a curse on Yoshitsune. However, the curse does not affect Yoshitsune and instead strikes Hidehira, who falls gravely ill on the tenth day of the twelfth month in the fifth year of Bunji (1189).

Well aware that he is dying, Hidehira sends an urgent message to Yoshitsune requesting his attendance. Yoshitsune rushes to the sick man's bedside, and Hidehira summons his five sons. In Yoshitsune's presence, he orders them to write an oath of fealty to Yoshitsune and presents them with a last will ordering them to maintain peaceful relations among themselves and to stand together in the face of the inevitable attack from Kamakura after his death. Above all, he enjoins them to honor his pledge of loyalty to Yoshitsune. On the twenty-first day of the same month, Hidehira dies in his ninety-seventh year.

Not one hundred days have passed before a message arrives from Kamakura, ordering the delivery of Yoshitsune's head and offering as bait the extension of the Ōshū Fujiwara's domain to include Kōzuke and five other provinces. Blinded by greed, the brothers agree to disobey their father's last testament. With the eldest, Nishikido no Tarō Yorihira, as their leader, they plot to attack Yoshitsune. Only one of them, Hidehira's third son, Izumi no Saburō Tadahira, remains loyal to his father's wishes. Enraged by his brother's plot, he storms out of the war council and returns to his own castle.

Fearing an alliance between their estranged brother and Yoshitsune, the remaining four brothers raise an army of more than three thousand and attack Tadahira at his Izumi Castle, hoping to force him to commit *seppuku*. Yoshitsune learns of this attack and dispatches Benkei to lead a force to assist Tadahira. Benkei sets out with a large group of retainers but, concerned for Yoshitsune's safety, returns to Takadachi.

Tadahira, who has no intention of going to war with his brothers, is completely unprepared. When the enemy breaks through the gates of his castle, he prepares to confront them weaponless, protected only by light armor. His wife, certain that he will be killed, begs him to slay their children first so that he may meet the enemy released from concern for the fate of those he leaves behind. Tadahira agrees and, with tears running down his face, stabs and kills his two sons, Hanaichi and Hanawaka.

Tadahira steps out onto the wide veranda of his private quarters to confront his brothers. Here he is joined by his wife, who is clad in a light green vest of mail and clasps a huge sword in a white scabbard. Tadahira's wife is the elder sister of Satō no Tsugunobu, who was killed in the battle at Yashima by an arrow shot by the governor of Nōtō, Taira no Noritsune, and her renown as an expert handler of the long sword had spread throughout the fifty-four districts of Ōshū.

Tadahira climbs to the top of the castle keep and lets loose a hail of arrows on the enemy army. When his arrows are exhausted, he and his wife plunge into the enemy ranks with swords flashing, killing all who stand in their way without discrimination. Finally, they retreat into the castle, and those who are left on the battlefield are awestruck, murmuring to each other that the display of martial valor they have witnessed could not have been effected by ordinary human beings.

Before the enemy can regroup, Tadahira orders two young servants to set fire to the castle. While the flames keep the attackers at bay, he and his wife sit down beside their two dead sons to face their own fate. Tadahira commits *seppuku*, and his wife swallows the point of her sword. Tadahira is in his thirty-second year, and his wife is four years younger. Thus the battle at Izumi Castle ends with the death of the loyal Tadahira, his brave wife, and all of their retainers.

# Kosode Soga 小袖曽我

## The Soga Brothers Receive *Kosode* Robes

Kanei-era edition. Large upright book. Two volumes. Seven illustrations, approximately 19.5 cm by 14.0 cm.

On their way to Minamoto no Yoritomo's encampment on the plain below Mount Fuji, where they have sworn to take revenge on Suketsune, their father's murderer, Soga no Jūrō Sukenari and Soga no Gorō Tokimune are overcome by the desire to see their mother one last time. As a child, Gorō had been sent by their mother to a temple on Hakone to become a priest and spend his life praying for the salvation of their father's soul. Burning with lust for revenge, however, Gorō was determined not to become a priest. When he came of age, he left the temple in Hakone, and then persuaded Hōjō no Tokimasa to perform his capping ceremony. Angered by his disobedience and his lack of filial piety toward his father, his mother had disinherited him. Thus, even though it is out of their way, the brothers are determined to visit their mother and plead with her to forgive Gorō.

Instructing Gorō to wait outside, Jūrō requests and is given permission to enter their mother's presence. He explains their mission at the foot of Mount Fuji and asks for her blessing. Saying that it is cold and snowy on the plain beneath Mount Fuji in winter, she gives him a new *kosode* robe to wear over his armor. Jūrō begs her to give one to Tokimune as well, but she replies that she has never heard the name Tokimune. Jūrō argues eloquently in his brother's defense, but she refuses to reply to his arguments. Now standing on the other side of a sliding panel that opens into the room, Gorō adds his own pleas for forgiveness, citing a number of cases of forgiveness for unfilial conduct in China and India.

Finally, their mother, who has endeavored so hard to hide her own feelings, opens the panel herself and, clinging to Gorō's knees, tearfully confesses that she has already forgiven him. The three of them hold a tiny banquet to celebrate Gorō's reinstatement, and, at his mother's request, Gorō performs his famous repertoire of dances. Their mother presents Gorō with a new *kosode* and confesses that the *kosode* Gorō had received the year before from his grandmother in Miura and his elder sister in Ninomiya had actually been from her. She had asked them to give them to Gorō, too ashamed of her weakness to receive him openly. The two brothers bid farewell, but, before departing, they slip two poems written on elegant paper into the space between the sliding panel. Here are their poems:

今日出でて　　　　We part today, lord, and
又も会はずは　　　If we do not meet again,
をぐるまの　　　　Understand, please, that
このはのうちに　　It is not in the spinning
なしと知れ君　　　Of the wheel that is this life.

As a remembrance for our next lives. Sukenari, in his twenty-first year.

| | |
|---|---|
| 秩父山 | On Mount Chichibu, |
| おろすあらしの | The autumn storms |
| はげしきに | Are cruel. |
| このみ散りなば | When the fruit has fallen, |
| ははいかにせん | What will become of the leaves? |

It is said that the bond between parent and child lasts only one lifetime, but I promise that we shall meet in paradise. Gorō Tokimune, in his nineteenth year.

Gorō's poem is particularly excellent, playing as it does on the name of a famous mountain. *Chichi*, the Japanese word for "father," is hidden in Mount Chichibu, and is a subtle allusion to the death of his father. *Konomi* can mean both "the fruit of the tree" and "one's own life," and similarly *ha* may refer to "the leaves of the tree" or to "mother."

They have their horses brought to the gate and prepare to continue their journey, as their mother, overcome with grief, sends them on their way.

Whipping their horses furiously they cross Mariko River and continue toward the plain below Mount Fuji. When they finally slow their pace, Gorō recalls the story of the goddesses at the temples in Izu and Hakone. Long, long ago in India, two princesses were cast adrift in a reed boat by their stepmother. Finally they drifted all the way across the ocean to Meragasaki in Izu. They became wandering nuns and for many years traveled around the country practicing devotions. In the end they were transformed into the goddesses of Izu and Hakone. As Gorō relates this story to while away the hours, they finally arrive at his former temple in Hakone.

Kan'ei-era old movable wooden type edition (*ko-katsujibon*). Published by Tsuruya Kyūbei. Large upright book. One volume. Nine illustrations, approximately 19.0 cm by 14.0 cm. This may be an elaboration of a similar episode that appears in chapter six of *Soga Monogatari*.

Wada no Yoshimori takes an excursion to Yamashita Station in the province of Sagami with a retinue of ninety-three mounted retainers. He takes lodgings at an inn called Kawara no Yado, for he has heard rumors that there is a courtesan working there whose beauty is unrivaled even in the capital, Oiso no Tora.

# *Wada Sakamori* 和田酒盛

## Wada Yoshimori's Drunken Banquet

Kanei-era old movable wooden type edition (*ko-katsujibon*). Published by Tsurugaya Kyūbei. Large upright book. One volume. Nine illustrations, approximately 19.0 cm by 14.0 cm.
*This story is an elaboration of a similar episode that appears in chapter six of* Soga Monogatari.

Wada no Yoshimori takes an excursion to Yamashita Station in the province of Sagami with a retinue of ninety-three mounted retainers. He takes lodgings at an inn called Kawara no Yado, for he has heard rumors that there is a courtesan working there whose beauty is unrivaled even in the capital, Ōiso no Tora.

He stages a magnificent banquet for all of his retainers, and the master of the inn sends thirty of the most beautiful women in his establishment to wait in attendance. Wada quickly realizes, however, that Tora is not among them and demands that she be summoned. It so happens that Tora's lover, Soga no Jūrō Sukenari, has come to say his last farewell before departing for Mount Fuji, and Tora refuses to leave his side, even after she has been called repeatedly. Torn between her filial duty to her mother, who insistently urges her to comply with Wada's requests, and her love for Jūrō, she finds herself in a hopeless dilemma.

Wada no Asahina Saburō Yoshihide, Yoshimori's eldest son, saves the situation by extending a polite invitation to join the banquet to both Tora and Jūrō. Impressed by Asahina's bearing and tact, Jūrō assents and urges Tora to accompany him. The three young people return to the banquet hall, and Jūrō is seated next to Yoshimori. Jūrō skillfully disguises his dislike of Yoshimori and the banquet quickly assumes a lively, jocular aspect. Suddenly, Tora's mother, who much prefers the powerful Yoshimori to the fugitive Jūrō, suggests a contest of love between the two. Hoping to win the favor of Yoshimori, she tells Tora to pour sake for the man of her choice. Again, Tora finds herself on the horns of a dilemma. If she follows her mother's wishes and pours for Yoshimori, it will anger Jūrō, her true lover and the father of her children. If she chooses Jūrō, however, she is certain to offend the volatile Yoshimori, who is in the company of ninety-three

He stages a magnificent banquet for all of his retainers, and the master of the inn sends thirty of the most beautiful women in his establishment to wait in attendance. Wada quickly realizes, however, that Tora is not among them and demands that she be summoned. It so happens that Tora's lover, Soga no Jūrō Sukenari, has come to say his last farewell before departing for Mount Fuji, and Tora refuses to leave his side, even after she has been called repeatedly. Torn between her filial duty to her mother, who insistently urges her to comply with Wada's requests, and her love for Jūrō, she finds herself in a hopeless dilemma.

Wada no Asahina Saburō Yoshihide, Yoshimori's eldest son, saves the situation by extending a polite invitation to join the banquet to both Tora and Jūrō. Impressed by Asahina's bearing and tact, Jūrō agrees, and urges Tora to accompany him. The three young people return to the banquet hall, and Jūrō is seated next to Yoshimori. Jūrō skillfully disguises his dislike of Yoshimori and the banquet quickly assumes a lively, jocular aspect.

Suddenly, Tora's mother, who much prefers the powerful Yoshimori to the fugitive Jūrō, suggests a contest of love between the two. Hoping to win the favor of Yoshimori, she tells Tora to pour *sake* for the man of her choice. Again, Tora finds herself on the horns of a dilemma. If she follows her mother's wishes and pours for Yoshimori, it will anger Jūrō, her true lover and the father of her children. If she chooses Jūrō, however, she is certain to offend the volatile Yoshimori, who is in the company of ninety-three strong retainers and well aware of Jūrō's perilous position. In desperation, she finally turns to fill Jūrō's cup. Brazenly, Jūrō tips his cup three times in the manner of a bridegroom. Yoshimori is enraged at this insult and demands that Jūrō leave the banquet. Jūrō's poorly concealed hatred of Yoshimori bursts out, and the two of them stand confronting each other, their hands hovering over the hilts of their swords.

Jūrō had ignored his brother's advice against visiting Tora's inn armed before their fateful encounter with Suketsune on Mount Fuji, and, now that he finds himself in this desperate confrontation, he is regretting his brash impetuosity. Strangely enough, at this very instant Gorō has a dream in which he sees his brother standing by his pillow trying to rouse him. He awakens and, still possessed by the intuition that his brother is in danger, hastily dons light armor, seizes his long sword, and rushes to Tora's inn, whipping his horse mercilessly.

Asahina Saburō, who has been ordered by his father to drive Jūrō out of the banquet hall, is aware that Gorō has arrived. Having once before been bested by Gorō, he is anxious for another chance to test his strength against his rival. Feigning ignorance of Gorō's presence on the other side of a *shōji* sliding panel, he attempts to calm his father by performing a repertoire of dances. Suddenly, he throws open the *shōji* and, catching hold of the tassets of Gorō's armor, tries to drag him into the banquet hall. Determined not to be outsmarted, Gorō resists, and three of his tassets come loose in the hands of Asahina. Considering this a sign of victory, Asahina proudly shows them to his father, and, placated, Yoshimori orders that the festivities be resumed. In high spirits, he invites Gorō to join the party and makes him a present of a fine light green corselet and a sword.

Finally the celebrations end, and Yoshimori has his horse brought to the veranda. Hoping to assuage to some degree his brother's embarrassment at being treated so rudely, Gorō criticizes Wada for mounting his horse before his guests. Afraid of Gorō's strength, Wada returns to his quarters leading his horse behind him.

among retainers and well aware of Goro's perilous position. In desperation, she finally turns to fill Jiro's cup. Uneasily, Jiro tips his own three times in the manner of a bridegroom. Yoshimori enraged at this insult and demand that they leave the banquet. Jiro's poorly concealed hatred of Yoshimori bursts out, and the two of them stand confronting each other, their hands hovering over the hilt of their swords.

Juro had ignored his brother's advice against visiting Toru un-armed before their fateful encounter with his pleasure on Mount Fuji, and now that he finds himself in this desperate confrontation, he is regretting his brash importunity. Strangely enough, at this very instant Goro has a dream in which he sees his brother standing by his pillow trying to rouse him. He awakens and, still possessed by the intuition that his brother is in danger, hastily dons high armor, seizes his long sword, and rushes to Toru's inn, whipping his horse mercilessly.

Asahina Saburo, who has been forbidden by his father to drive Juro out of the banquet hall, is aware that Goro has arrived. Having once before been bested by Goro, he is anxious for another chance to test his strength against his rival. Feigning ignorance of Goro's presence on the other side of a wall sliding panel, he attempts to calm his father by performing a repertoire of dances. Suddenly, he throws open the shutter and, catching hold of the tassel of Goro's armor, tries to drag him into the banquet hall. Determined not to be unarmed, Goro resists, and three of his tassels come loose in the hands of Asahina. Considering this a sign of victory, Asahina proudly bows then to his father, and, placated, Yoshimori orders that the festivities be resumed. In high spirits, he invites Goro to join the party and makes him a present of a fine light green corselet and a sword. Finally the celebrations end, and Yoshimori has his horse brought to the veranda. Hoping to assuage to some degree his brother's embarrassment at being treated so rudely, Goro criticizes Wada for mounting his horse before his guests. Afraid of Goro's strength, Wada retires to his quarter, leading his horse behind him.

# Taishokukan 大織冠

## The Adventures of the Taishokukan

Kanei 12 (1635) edition. Large upright book. Two volumes. Eleven illustrations, approximately 19.5 cm by 15.0 cm.

Fujiwara no Kamatari is the grandson of the Kasuga Myōjin, the guardian deity of the Fujiwara. Even while a boy, he wins great distinction by crushing a rebellion led by Soga no Iruka, and he is rewarded with the coveted office of Taishokukan. He confines himself in the sanctuary of the Kasuga Myōjin to pray for the good fortunes of his family and emerges to order the construction of Kōfuku-ji.

The Taishokukan's first daughter becomes the consort of Emperor Shōmu (reigned 724–49), and, because of her great beauty and intelligence, she is known as the Empress Kōmyō. She is rivaled only by her younger sister, Kōhaku, who is famous even in the courts of China and India. Indeed, Emperor Tai-zong is so moved by the stories of her unparalleled beauty that he falls hopelessly in love. He sends an emissary to Japan with a marriage proposal. Kamatari refuses, but Tai-zong, determined not to be frustrated in his attempt to win this priceless jewel, sends a second emissary. Emperor Shōmu intercedes, and Kamatari finally agrees. Overjoyed, Tai-zong sends three hundred ships to escort Kōhaku to the Tang capital.

Kōhaku wins the love of the Tang people and, in order to impress the Japanese with the splendor of the Tang capital, she resolves to make a donation to Kōfuku-ji. She prepares a gift of priceless gems, including the legendary Mukei pearl, and charges the great General Unsō with the task of delivering the treasure to Japan. Unfortunately, the Eight Kings of the Sea Dragon Kingdom learn of this mission and attempt to steal the gems by stirring up a great sea storm. Yasha Rasetsu intervenes to calm the storm.

The sea dragon kings appeal to the Ashura gods, who attack Unsō's fleet with a force of tens of thousands of Ashura. After a fierce battle, however, Unsō defeats them and makes his escape. Angered at this defeat, the dragon king Nanda devises a crafty scheme. He summons Kohisa, the most beautiful of the ladies-in-waiting serving the dragon princess Otohime, and, after careful plotting, she is set adrift on the sea in a reed boat. As planned, she is rescued by Unsō. She tells him the carefully fabricated story that she was set adrift by the King of Khithai, after being slandered by those jealous of her status as the king's favorite. Unsō is completely taken in and allows his guard to drop. Kohisa steals the Mukei pearl and disappears. In despair of recovering the pearl, Unsō is forced to content himself with delivering the remaining jewels to Nara.

Determined to recover the Mukei pearl, the Taishokukan himself travels to Fusazaki. He soon finds that he too is powerless against the dragon kings and returns to Nara. However, the clever Taishokukan quickly devises a new plan and sets off again for Fusazaki. There he seeks out an expert *ama* diver and woos her persistently until she becomes his lover. Three years later, she bears him a son. Now Kamatada finally reveals his true identity and tells her of his plan to recover the Mukei pearl.

After searching the ocean floor for seven days, the *ama* diver discovers that the pearl is being kept in the dragon palace itself. Kamatada now puts his plan into action. Aware that the dragon gods are fond of music as succor against the five sorrows and the three fevers, he gathers all the boats in the Fusazaki harbor and has them arrayed with gorgeous decorations. He sends to the capital for the finest court musicians and stages a wonderful performance of music and dance aboard the assembled ships. The dragon gods appear with all their retainers, and soon are entranced by the performance. In the meantime, the *ama* penetrates the dragon palace and steals the Mukei pearl. Unfortunately, she is discovered by the minor dragon gods left behind to guard the pearl, and they give chase. The *ama* slashes open her chest and conceals the pearl inside the wound. She makes her escape but dies in Kamatada's arms. He removes the pearl from the sword wound and, upon his return to Kōfuku-ji, has it embedded between the eyebrows of the great Buddha he has had enshrined at Kōfuku-ji. The son born to him by the *ama* is given the name Fusamae.

## The Story of Manjū

Kan'ei-era edition. Large upright book. Two volumes. Ten illustrations. approximately 19.0 cm by 14.5 cm.

Tada no Manjū is the son of Minamoto no Mitsunaka, who was known as Rokuson-ō (Rikyū Sixth Grandson) because his own father had been the sixth son of the Emperor Seiwa (reigned 858-76). He is the most skillful warrior in the land, unrivaled in his use perhaps with bow and arrow. One day, however, he awakens to the transience of life and becomes a devout Buddhist. Manjū decides to have his youngest son, Bijōmaru, devote himself to prayers for his father's next life. He sends the boy to Nakayama-dera in Settsu. Bijōmaru detests his studies and, determined not to spend his life as a priest, spends all his time practicing martial arts, forcing the other temple pages to act as his partners.

# *Manjū* 満仲

## The Story of Manjū

Kanei-era edition. Large upright book. Two volumes. Ten illustrations, approximately 19.0 cm by 14.5 cm.

Tada no Manjū is the son of Minamoto no Tsunemoto, who was known as Rokuson-ō (King Sixth Grandson) because his own father had been the sixth son of the Emperor Seiwa (reigned 858–76). He is the most skillful warrior in the land, unrivaled in his expertise with bow and arrow. One day, however, he awakens to the transience of life and becomes a devout Buddhist. Manjū decides to have his youngest son, Bijomaru, devote himself to prayers for his father's next life. He sends the boy to Nakayama-dera in Settsu. Bijomaru detests his studies and, determined not to spend his life as a priest, spends all his time practicing martial arts, forcing the other temple pages to act as his partners.

Manjū knows nothing of this and, after several years have passed, summons Bijomaru for a visit. He asks his son to recite the Lotus Sutra and is stunned to find that Bijomaru cannot read a single word. Enraged, he draws his sword and attempts to kill his son, but Bijomaru has not neglected his study of martial arts and, evading his father's attack with wonderful finesse, he makes his escape. He appeals to an old minister of the court, Nakatsukasa no Nakamitsu, who hides him in his mansion.

Manjū learns of Bijomaru's whereabouts and sends Nakamitsu a magnificent sword that has been passed down in the family for generations, bidding him use it to strike off Bijomaru's head. His loyalties utterly divided, Nakamitsu resolves to kill his own son, Kōjumaru, who is the same age as Bijomaru. Like Bijomaru, Kōjumaru had been sent to a temple in his eighth year to become a priest. On account of his intelligence and extraordinary good looks, he has quickly risen to the rank of tutor to the other temple pages. Overjoyed at the prospect of seeing his parents after a long separation, Kōjumaru immediately sets off for home at double pace with Nakamitsu's messenger.

He arrives to find his father in tears. Finally he understands the nature of the summons. Explaining his dilemma, Nakamitsu begs his son to consent to die in Bijomaru's place. Young though he is, Kōjumaru immediately recognizes the wisdom of his father's stratagem and agrees. After a final meeting with his mother, at which he carefully conceals the fate that awaits him, he composes the following poem in preparation for death:

| 君 が た め | I exchange my life |
| 命 に か は る | For my lord's. |
| 後 の 世 の | Shining through the darkness |
| 闇 を ば 照 ら せ | Of the afterlife, |
| 山 の 端 の 月 | The moon rising from the mountain. |

Nakamitsu tearfully beheads his son and presents the head to Manjū.

Bijomaru learns of this deception and attempts to commit suicide. He is restrained by Nakamitsu and his wife, who persuade him to return to the priesthood and send him to Mount Hiei. He becomes the disciple of Eshin, founder of the Eshin-in monastery, and devotes himself diligently to his studies. In his eighteenth year, he shaves his head and takes the name Egaku of Eshin-in. In his twenty-fourth year, he reveals his true identity to Eshin, and they set off together to visit his father.

They arrive in Tada, and Eshin Sōzu calls on Manjū. He sternly rebukes Manjū for his behavior and, leaving Egaku behind in Tada, returns to Mount Hiei. Manjū's wife has become blind as a result of her deep grief at what she believes was the death of her son, and Egaku prays day and night for the restoration of her vision. A miraculous golden light springs from the great Buddha on Mount Hiei and shines on his mother's forehead. Immediately, her vision is restored. Egaku reveals his true identity, and tells his parents the whole story of the deception and of his return to the priesthood. After this tearful reunion, Manjū gives Nakamitsu half of his domain and orders the construction of a new temple, Shōtō-ji, at which he commissions daily devotions for the salvation of Kōjumaru's soul. The image he has constructed there is called Chigo Monju (the Temple Page's Manjusri).

# Yuriwaka Daijin 百合若大臣

## Great Minister Yuriwaka Defeats the King of the Devils

Kanei-era edition. Large upright book. One volume (only the first of two volumes is extant). Seven illustrations, approximately 19.0 cm by 14.5 cm.

During the reign of Emperor Saga (809–823), the Minister of the Left, Kinmitsu, has devotions performed at Hase-dera in Yamato, entreating Kannon to bless him with a son. Finally his wife bears him a son, and he calls the boy Yuriwaka. In his sixteenth year, Yuriwaka succeeds his father and marries the daughter of the Great Councilor Sanjō no Mibu.

At about the same time, Takejizai-ten, the king of the devils, resolves to attack Japan, the protector of the Buddhist Law. He raises a fleet of forty thousand ships, manned by the Mukuri devils of the land of Muko. He appoints Ryōshō, Kuwasui, Tobukumo, and Hashirukumo as admirals and orders them to attack Japan at Hakata in Tsukushi (Kyushu). The fleet attacks Hakata, and a hail of cannon fire and poisoned arrows rains down on the city.

The gods of Japan hold a council on Takamagahara, the plain of heaven, and send an oracle instructing the court to appoint Yuriwaka Daijin as their general and to send him immediately against Takejizai-ten. On the eighth day of the second month of the seventh year of Kōnin (816), Yuriwaka sets off for Hakata with a fleet of thirty thousand ships, carrying a gigantic iron bow. The Mukuri devils are terrified of Yuriwaka and retreat. Yuriwaka returns in triumph, and the court rewards him by making him the governor of all of Tsukushi. They commission him to lead a fleet of eighty thousand ships against the Mukuri devils in the land of Muko.

Yuriwaka sets sail, but encounters a fleet of forty thousand Muko ships at Chikuragaoki, the ocean border between Japan and Tang China. After a sea war lasting three years, Yuriwaka finally defeats the Mukuri devils. On the return voyage, however, he puts in at Genkai Island, where he is betrayed by the Beppu brothers, once his most trusted retainers. While their leader is napping, the Beppu brothers seize the fleet and leave him stranded on Genkai Island.

On their return to the capital, the Beppu brothers fabricate the story that Yuriwaka has been killed by enemy arrows. Claiming the honors of the victory for themselves, they take over the governorship of Tsukushi. Brazenly, they both begin sending love letters to Yuriwaka's wife, but she sees through their schemes and becomes convinced that they have betrayed her husband. Helpless against them, she resigns herself and makes donations from Yuriwaka's treasury to various temples. Also in his memory, she releases his hunting dogs and his thirty-two favorite falcons. Among them is the most loyal of Yuriwaka's falcons, the horned hawk Midorimaru. Relying on his keen instincts, Midorimaru flies to his master on Genkai Island.

Overcome with joy, Yuriwaka breaks off a leaf and writes a message to his wife in his own blood. Midorimaru bears the message back to Yuriwaka's wife. She resolves to send Yuriwaka an inkstone and a brush. However, the inkstone is too heavy for Midorimaru, and after flying three days and three nights to Genkai Island he falls to the

beach dying. Yuriwaka despairs that communications have once more been broken.

Perhaps because of his wife's prayers at the Hachiman Shrine in Usa, a boat from Iki Island gets lost in a storm and is driven to Genkai Island. Yuriwaka persuades the islanders to take him to Tsukushi.

The Beppu brothers learn that the Iki islanders have brought a strange man with them and have him seized. They turn him over to an old man called Kadowaki. Not long ago, Kadowaki had remonstrated with the Beppu brothers when they decided in their frustration to have Yuriwaka's wife bound and thrown into a lake, finally offering his own daughter as a substitute.

Yuriwaka takes the name Kokemaru and becomes the old man's servant. When all the greater and lesser lords of the land visit Tsukushi for the New Year celebration, Yuriwaka appears before them with his iron bow and arrows. Demonstrating his skills as an archer, he reveals his true identity. The elder Beppu is put to death on the spot, while the younger is subjected to cruel torture.

Yuriwaka and his loyal wife are rejoined, and, in his joy, Yuriwaka pledges that he will put the Hachiman Shrine at Usa under his personal protection. He returns to the capital and is made commander in chief of the emperor's army and navy.

120

# Otogizōshi

御伽草子

# Jūnidan Sōshi 十二段草子

## The Story of Lady Jōruri in Twelve Stages

Shōhō 3 (1646) edition. Large upright book. Three volumes bound into one (some leaves missing). Nine illustrations, approximately 19.0 cm by 13.5 cm.

At Yahagi Station in Mikawa, there is a lady of great beauty and refinement, unparalleled in Japan, and even in the courts of China. She is called Jōruri Gozen. Her father is the provincial governor, and her mother, before her marriage, had been a courtesan of unrivaled fame. They were so rich that gold and silver are as the froth in the surf, but for many years their happiness had been marred because their marriage was childless. Year after year they had made offerings to the Yakushi Buddha at Hōrai-ji on Mount Hōrai, and finally the Buddha had answered their prayers and brought about the birth of the beautiful Jōruri.

The story of Lady Jōruri and Minamoto no Yoshitsune takes place when the young Yoshitsune is on his way to Ōshū with Kichiji Nobutaka. He has gone through his capping ceremony but is still traveling as a temple page. At Yahagi Station, they pass a splendid mansion, and Yoshitsune, wondering what sort of people could live in such a place, ventures to peer inside. Suddenly he hears the strains of a wonderfully refined *koto*. Drawn by the music, he makes bold to enter and finds himself transported into the most elegant surroundings conceivable. Water shimmers in a lovely stream surrounded by an elegant garden, and wonderful buildings greet his eyes whichever way he turns. It is a sight, he feels, that surpasses even the great mansions in the capital.

Within one of the buildings opening onto the garden, Lady Jōruri and her ladies in waiting, who are only slightly less beautiful than Lady Jōruri herself, are playing a lovely repertoire that includes songs no longer heard even at court. He notices, however, that they do not seem to have a *yokofue* flute. He takes out his own flute, the legendary Aoba, and begins to play a song called "Sōfuren" (Thoughts of My Mate), one of the secret songs of the Imperial Bureau of Music.

Lady Jōruri sends one of her ladies to discover the identity of this marvelous musician. The lady returns to say that he seems to be a temple page. Lady Jōruri is aware that a number of courtiers and high-ranking Minamoto warriors have fled the capital and, suspecting that the musician is one of them, sends a lady called Tomamo no Mae to inquire again. Tomamo no Mae returns to report that the young man is dressed in splendid attire and certainly has the bearing of a man of noble birth. Her suspicions confirmed, Lady Jōruri sends each of her seven ladies in turn to invite Yoshitsune to join them.

They play a number of songs together, and then the ladies take turns questioning Yoshitsune about music. Besieged with questions concerning the music of the court, Yoshitsune nevertheless answers each of their questions with great subtlety, demonstrating his profound knowledge. After this gay banquet, Yoshitsune returns to his lodgings. Unable to forget the image of Lady Jōruri, however, he returns again to the mansion and enters by stealth, searching out her private quarters. He makes his way past seven standing screens and eight hanging screens, finally discovering the lady asleep. Marshaling all his wit and subtle charm, he attempts to seduce her, but Lady Jōruri is his equal, and their elegant dialogue continues deep into the night. In the end, of course, she succumbs to his entreaties, and the bond of love is sealed between them.

On the following day, Yoshitsune forces himself to part with his new love and rejoins Kichiji on the road to Ōshū. At Fukiage no Ura, however, he falls gravely ill and is left on the beach to die. Yoshitsune's divine protector, Hachiman, appears before Lady Jōruri and tells her of his plight. She rushes to Fukiage. Yoshitsune has died, but the gods are moved by Lady Jōruri's prayers, and miraculously he returns from the dead. Yoshitsune reveals his true identity and promises that they will meet again. Tearfully they part, and Yoshitsune rushes to rejoin Kichiji's caravan.

The story of Lady Jōruri was told over and over by wandering monks and nuns, and her name now denotes the mysterious chanting styles of the Jōruri theater.

# Chikubujima no Honji 竹生島の本地
## The Legend of Chikubujima

Genna-era (1615–24) edition. Medium-size upright book (*hanshibon*). Old movable wooden type edition. One volume. Four illustrations, approximately 17.5 cm by 13.5 cm. From the collection of Yokoyama Ai.

The legend of Chikubujima is set in the not-too-distant past. In the city of Ichizaka in Yamato, there is a beautiful lady of good birth who lost her father when she was still quite young and is now leading an impoverished life with her mother. One day, a priest from nearby Ichizaka-dera appears at her door and rebukes her for her unfilial conduct, admonishing her that she must provide for memorial services for her father, even if it means selling herself. Deeply moved by the priest's admonition, she awaits an opportunity, and, in the thirteenth year after her father's death, she sells herself to an Ōshū merchant for fifty pieces of gold. She makes arrangements for memorial devotions for her father and confesses everything to her mother. After a tearful parting, she sets off for Ōshū with the merchant.

They arrive at the merchant's home in the district of Adachi, and he orders his wife to treat the lady with the utmost respect. In fact, however, he is concealing a ghastly plan. In a pond deep in the mountains near the village, there lives a gigantic serpent, and it is the custom in this village to offer the serpent a human sacrifice once every year. The merchant's own daughter has been chosen as the sacrificial victim for this year, and he hopes to substitute the lady from Ichizaka in her place. The lady is horrified when she hears of this plan but, having sold herself to the merchant, resigns herself to her fate.

On the day of the sacrificial ceremony, she dresses herself in twelve layers of kimono and, clutching a set of scrolls containing the Lotus Sutra, calmly takes her position on the dais that has been prepared near the edge of the pond. Soon the surface of the pond begins to whirl and from its murky waters appears a huge serpent with sixteen horns. As the serpent approaches the sacrificial dais, his bright red tongue flashes out to wrap itself around the helpless lady. Suddenly she raises her hand, bidding the serpent wait for just a moment, and then begins to read from the scrolls bearing the Lotus Sutra. As she intones each scroll, she calls out the name of the person she is praying for: the first scroll for her father, the second scroll for her mother, the third and the fourth scroll for the merchant, and, suddenly, the fifth scroll for the serpent himself. The fifth scroll of the Lotus Sutra, the *Daibabon*, tells the story of a dragon princess who died in her eighth year, and how, through the mercy of Kannon, she was granted salvation and became a Buddha. Declaring that this chapter of the Lotus Sutra will save the serpent from the torments of his lowly status on the scale of existence, the lady places it on his head. The serpent immediately lowers his horns and sinks below the surface of the pond.

A short time passes as the spectators stand in mute awe, and then the serpent rises to the surface again with a thousand pieces of gold resting on his horns. Announcing that the power of the sutra he has heard has freed him from the torment of being imprisoned in the body of a snake and that he will now be able to achieve salvation, he offers the gold as a present to the lady. Bidding her mount his enormous head, he flies her in an instant back to her home in far-off Ichizaka. She is reunited with her mother, and they live together in happiness. Near the end of her life as a mortal human being, the lady reveals herself as Benzai-ten, and on his death the serpent is reincarnated as the Kannon of Ichizaka.

# Fuji no Hitoana 富士の人穴

## The Hole of Man at Mount Fuji

Kanei 4 (1627) edition. Large upright book. Two volumes. Sixteen illustrations, approximately 19.5 cm by 14.0 cm.

On the third day of the fourth month of the first year of Shōji (1199), the Kamakura shogun, Minamoto no Yoriie, orders Wada no Koheita to investigate the hole of man at Mount Fuji (*Fuji no hitoana*). Wada travels to Mount Fuji, and searches out the entrance to the cave. He ventures inside and, after leaping over the heads of countless fire-breathing serpents, he finds himself deep in the interior. Here he encounters a beautiful lady weaving on a loom. She casts a baleful glance at him and commands him to leave. Suddenly he is encompassed by a blast of magical wind and finally recovers his senses to find himself outside the mysterious cave. He returns to Kamakura to report his experiences to Yoriie.

More and more intrigued, Yoriie offers a huge treasure as reward for anyone brave enough to repeat Wada's journey in quest of the secret of the cave. For some time, no one accepts this challenge, but finally Nitta no Shirō Tadatsuna, who is also known as Shirō Tadatsune, steps forward. Promising to return in seven days, he sets off for Mount Fuji. He arrives at the cave and enters carrying thirty bright torches. He walks some distance down the cave without incident, and so, drawing his sword, he resolves to venture further. Suddenly he emerges into an underground world of blinding light, dominated by a magnificent palace that rivals in splendor the palace of the Tang emperor. There is also a huge golden temple, and the droplets of water dripping from its eaves seem at once to echo the wind, to tinkle like bells, and to reverberate with the words of holy sutras. To the north there is a lovely lotus pond, and for a moment he stands in awe of this unearthly panorama.

Trembling with fear, he approaches the island in the center of the pond, and the Asama Buddha appears before him in the form of a gigantic serpent, demanding his swords. Once Shirō Tadatsune is unarmed, Asama changes form again and appears as a priest in his sixteenth or seventeenth year. Noting that human beings know nothing of the worlds of hell or paradise, he offers to act as a guide for Shirō Tadatsune.

From Sainokawara, the purgatory reserved for infants who die in birth, they cross Sanzu River to Mount Shide, the mountain of death, and finally proceed to the various Buddhist hells. As the priest expounds upon the inexorable laws of Karma, Shirō Tadatsune is forced to witness the writhing and suffering of the tortured sinners. Finally they reach the office of Enma, where the god of death makes the sinners stand before the mirror of Jōhari, in which the sins of their lives as mortals are reflected in painfully accurate detail.

From hell, he is led to paradise, where he is shown the palaces of Amida, Shaka, the Yakushi Buddha, the Bodhisattva Seishi, Jizō, and all of the various minor Bodhisattvas, and made to worship at their shrines. Finally the monk writes out a description of the various aspects of heaven and hell in a book. He gives it to Shirō Tadatsune, commanding him to conceal it over his heart inside his armor. He further commands him to wait until his thirtieth year and then to climb Mount Izu and reveal its contents to the

Japanese people, warning him that if he disobeys these commands he will not only lose his own life but Yoritō, his lord, will be sacrificed as well. With these words, Shirō Tadatsune finds himself back at the entrance to the cave.

Saitō Tadatsune returns to Kamakura to report to Yoritō. When news of his miraculous return spreads, all the lords both great and lowly gather at Yoritō's court to hear the story of his quest. Pressed by Yoritō to recount the details of his adventure, Shirō Tadatsune finds himself in a dilemma: Finally he tells himself that he cannot disobey his lord even if it means suffering punishment from the Asura Buddha, and he begins to speak of the Mount Fuji inferno. Suddenly a profound voice from heaven booms over the hall saying that the lives of both Tadatsune and Yoritō are forfeit. Cursed by the Asura Buddha, Shirō Tadatsune is dead before the sun has sunk below the horizon.

Japanese people, warning him that if he disobeys these commands he will not only lose his own life but Yoriie, his lord, will be sacrificed as well. With these words, Shirō Tadatsune finds himself back at the entrance to the cave.

Shirō Tadatsune returns to Kamakura to report to Yoriie. When news of his miraculous return spreads, all the lords both great and lowly gather at Yoriie's court to hear the story of his quest. Pressed by Yoriie to recount the details of his adventure, Shirō Tadatsune finds himself in a dilemma. Finally he tells himself that he can not disobey his lord, even if it means suffering punishment from the Asama Buddha, and he begins to speak of the Mount Fuji inferno. Suddenly a profound voice from heaven booms over the hall, saying that the lives of both Tadatsune and Yoriie are forfeit. Cursed by the Asama Buddha, Shirō Tadatsune is dead before the sun has sunk below the horizon.

# Kumano no Honji 熊野の本地

## The Legend of Kumano

Kanei-era edition. Large upright book. Three volumes. Sixty-three illustrations, approximately 20.0 cm by 15.0 cm.

*This edition is particularly interesting because its composition is based on that of an old picture scroll (emakimono). It is highly illustrated, and in many places illustrations run for several pages in the style of the scroll.*

King Zenzai of the kingdom of Makada (Magadha) in India, in deep despair because he has no heir to succeed him, consults a learned diviner, who advises him to assemble a harem of one thousand wives. The last of the one thousand beautiful women selected is the daughter of the Great Minister of the Central Gate. Because of her lowly birth, she is not admitted into the women's quarters in the palace but is installed at one of the king's distant residences, the Palace of the Five Sufferings. Forgotten by the king, she passes six long years without a single visit from him. Saddened by his neglect, the lady appeals to the the Kannon of Eleven Aspects, who answers her prayers by causing the king to suddenly remember her. Finally the king visits the lady and, overcome by her matchless beauty, makes her his favorite. Soon she is with child, and the king's love becomes even more intense.

The king spends all of his time at the Palace of the Five Sufferings, and now it is the turn of the remaining nine hundred and ninety-nine wives to feel the pangs of neglect. Inflamed by jealousy, they conspire to have a soothsayer predict falsely that the child to be born will be a grotesque devil, that he will bring destruction to the country, and that he will murder his parents. The king, however, is completely unmoved by this prophecy. The wives at court then assemble a great force composed of the ugliest hags in the kingdom, and, dressing them as devils, force their way into the Palace of the Five Sufferings, threatening to kill everyone in sight if the king refuses to give up his lover. Terrified by these apparently supernatural devils, the king tearfully leaves the palace and returns to the court.

The jealous wives seize this opportunity to issue an order under the king's signature commanding that the lady of the Palace of the Five Sufferings be taken to a place deep in the mountains and killed. The warriors who receive this order eagerly arrest the lady and set off for a distant place in the mountains. After traveling seven days and seven nights, they reach the foothills of Mount Chiko and prepare for the execution at a place called Tora no Iwaya. After repeated attempts to behead the lady, however, they find it impossible. They try shooting her with arrows, but the arrows fall around her shattered. Calmly, the lady turns to the awestruck warriors and tells them that, indeed, she cannot be killed until her child is born. She quietly folds her hands and prays to the Buddhas and gods to hasten the arrival of the child. Soon a male child of brilliant countenance emerges from her womb. After explaining to the baby what the future holds for him, the lady seizes a sword and cuts off her hair. She offers it to the mountain gods and appeals to them to protect the child. As she begins to chant the name of the Amida Buddha, she is finally beheaded. However, her body clutches the infant to her breast, nursing

the baby boy even in death. Having carried out their bloody mission, the stout warriors are in tears as they carry her head back to the capital.

Left in the mountains, the boy drinks the milk from his murdered mother's breast and is later protected by tigers and other wild beasts until he reaches his third year. At the base of the mountain lives a saintly ascetic called Jigen Shōnin. Jigen hears strange stories of a boy who lives with tigers and wild beasts and seeks him out, bringing him to live in his own rude hut at the foot of the mountain. As the boy grows taller and stronger, he excels in his studies of the holy scriptures, and word of his precocious talents reaches as far as the capital. When the boy is in his sixth year, the king, who has fallen grievously ill, hears of a remarkable page in the service of Jigen and sends a messenger to request that the boy perform prayers for his recovery.

The boy performs devotions for the king, and the king's health is immediately restored. The king presses the boy to speak of his origins, and the boy relates the story of his mother's murder and his own wanderings in the wilderness. Overjoyed, the king prepares to abdicate in favor of his long-lost son, but the prince explains that he has left this world to become a wandering ascetic and devote his life to prayers for his mother's soul.

The prince gathers the head and bones of his mother and entreats Jigen to perform the secret rites that will restore her to life. Jigen assents to this request, and the lady of the Palace of the Five Sufferings is returned to life in all her former beauty. Disgusted with what has happened in his kingdom, the king mounts a flying palanquin with his beloved wife, his son, and the old sage Jigen, and they fly to Japan. After wandering all over the country, they finally cease their travels near the banks of Otonashi River in the province of Kii, where the king is transformed into the Great Buddha of Kumano-dera.

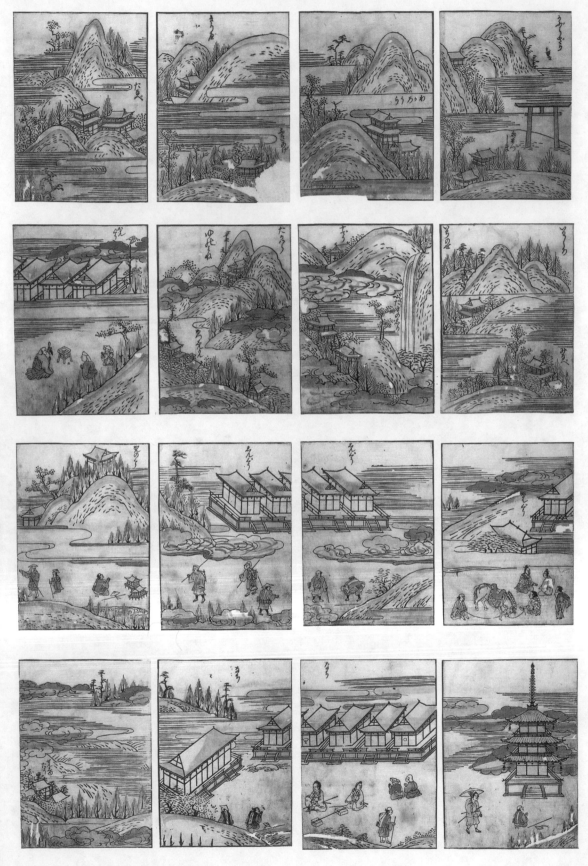

# Bunshō Sōshi 文正草子

## The Story of Bunshō's Good Fortune

Jōō 2 (1653) edition. Large upright book. Two volumes. Twelve illustrations, approximately 20.0 cm by 16.0 cm. From the collection of Yokoyama Ai. (For a complete translation of *Bunshō Sōshi*, see James Araki, "Bunshō the Saltmaker," *Monumenta Nipponica*, vol. 38, no. 3, Autumn 1983.)

The chief priest of the Kashima Shrine in Hitachi is a fabulously wealthy man called the Daigūji. Among his many servants is a man called Bunda, who has served him honestly for many years. On a sudden whim, however, the Daigūji decides to test Bunda and, on a transparent pretext, sends him away. Though he had never dreamed of anything but to serve his master faithfully until the end of his days, Bunda has no choice but to leave. He finds work with a salt merchant in a place called Tsunooka no Iso.

After several years of loyal service to his new master, Bunda begs the man to help him establish his own business. His master agrees readily and gives him two of his own salt boiling pots. Perhaps because of divine intervention, Bunda's pots suddenly begin to produce huge quantities of salt. Moreover, his salt is soon known far and wide for its mysterious medicinal effects. Bunda becomes fabulously wealthy, with a large mansion and countless storehouses. He changes his name to Bunshō Tsuneoka, increases the number of his storehouses, and soon has many servants of his own. Finally, he feels rich enough to marry, but, even after several years, he and his wife remain childless.

The Daigūji hears of Bunda's success and invites him for a visit. He reveals his true feelings, and suggests that Bunshō appeal to the god of the shrine, Kashima Myōjin. Bunshō visits the shrine regularly and makes generous offerings from his many treasure houses. He has a dream in which he encounters Kashima Myōjin and receives two lotus flowers. In due course, his wife bears him two beautiful daughters, and he gives them the names Renge Gozen and Hachisu Gozen.

The two girls grow up to become unparalleled beauties of great wit and intelligence. Bunshō is showered with marriage proposals from the great lords of the east, but his daughters have high ambitions, and he is forced to refuse these proposals one after the other. The Daigūji himself proposes a match between Renge Gozen and his eldest son, but this too is refused. Finally, the governor of Hitachi presses Bunshō to arrange a marriage with Renge Gozen for himself. She refuses and, when he attempts to use force, threatens to commit suicide.

It so happens that the regent, who is the most powerful man at court, has a son of the second court rank who is called the Middle Captain. One day, the Middle Captain is speaking to the governor of Hitachi and is told of the beauty of Bunshō's daughters. Enchanted, he resolves to visit Hitachi himself, and is encouraged by three of his young retainers. They disguise themselves as merchants and set out along the Tōkaidō for Hitachi.

Finally they arrive in Kashima and, at a place near Bunshō's mansion, set up business selling beautiful kimono and other things they have brought from the capital. With their refined Kyoto accents, they are enormously successful and soon win Bunshō's friendship. He offers them lodgings in his own mansion, and the Middle Captain seizes this opportunity to approach Bunshō's daughter Renge Gozen. Filling a box with beautiful things from the capital, the Middle Captain sends it to her with a suggestive note inside.

Renge Gozen is deeply impressed with the elegance of his handwriting and the grace of his message and, for the first time, finds herself attracted by this young suitor. Sometime later, the four young men stage a performance of court music at the Kashima Shrine. Bunshō finds the performance so admirable that he invites them to perform again for his daughters. As they play, a gust of wind catches the screen behind which the daughters are secluded, and the Middle Captain and Renge Gozen catch a glance of each other. That evening, the Middle Captain steals into the ladies' chamber, and the bond of love is sealed.

The Daigūji comes to visit Bunshō, and the Middle Captain takes this opportunity to shed his merchant's garments and announce his true identity. Astonished, the Daigūji hurries off to assemble a proper entourage. The Middle Captain and Renge Gozen declare their love, and together they depart for the capital, where she becomes his wife. The younger sister, Hachisu Gozen, becomes the consort of the emperor and the mother of his heir. Bunshō is summoned to the capital, where he is given court rank and lives a life of luxury until his death at the grand old age of one hundred years.

# Hioke no Sōshi 火桶の草子

## The Story of a Broken Brazier

Kanei-era edition. Large upright book. One volume. Eight illustrations, approximately 19.5 cm by 14.0 cm. From the collection of Yokoyama Ai.

This is the story of an old man and his wife who lived a long, long time ago.

The old man and his wife live in a poor hut constructed of brushwood in a certain place deep in the wilderness. The old man loves nothing more than to sit at his brazier, and he spends night and day there warming his knees as he composes poetry in the classical court style. As a result, he neglects his wife, and the old woman becomes increasingly jealous of the old man's brazier.

One day, when the old man has gone out to collect firewood, she vents her jealousy on the brazier with a stream of angry recriminations and finally splits it in half with the old man's broad axe. Much to her surprise, the brazier begins to bleed, and soon there is bright red blood flying everywhere.

When the old man returns from the mountains and sees what has happened, he is enraged and begins to beat his wife mercilessly with his staff. She bursts into tears and threatens to leave the old man, pouring out all her resentment at being neglected by him in favor of the brazier. The old man responds by berating her for the meanness of her jealousy, citing the five duties of women and recounting the story from Tang China of the mother

of the orchid tree. Not so easily defeated, the old woman argues that she did not break the brazier just out of jealousy but also because she was afraid it might cause a fire.

This starts the old man off on another tirade about how the old woman thinks of nothing but domestic practicalities while he is more inclined to the pursuit of elegant pastimes. He cites the famous preface to the *Kokinshū*, in which Ki no Tsurayuki argues that even bush warblers and frogs create poetry, and that poetry has the power to calm the spirits of all the gods and devils. He launches into a lecture on the imperial collections of poetry and the *Hyakunin Isshu*. Finally, he concludes triumphantly with the story of how Fujiwara no Shunzei himself had composed poetry at his brass brazier.

The old lady responds by reciting anecdotes about feminine jealousy from such great classics as the *Tale of Genji* and the *Tale of the Heike*. But finally she accepts defeat and begs the old man's forgiveness for breaking his brazier. The old man, however, is astonished at this demonstration of her profound knowledge of the classics and impressed with the gentle sincerity of her apology. In the end, he says that everything in this world is but a veil of dreams and suggests that they spend their time in the future praying for happiness in their next lives. Thus the old man and the old woman are reconciled, and they live happily ever after.

# Tengu no Dairi 天狗の内裏

## Yoshitsune's Visit to the Court of the Great Tengu

Shōhō era (1644–48) edition. Large upright book. Two volumes (some leaves missing). Eleven illustrations, approximately 18.8 cm by 14.8 cm.

Minamoto no Onzōshi Ushiwaka is sent to the temple on Mount Kurama in his sixth year to become a priest and perform prayers for his father's salvation. He devotes himself to study and, because he is a manifestation of Bishamon, is able to master all of the sutras and the great classics at a single reading. Soon he has no rival in the profundity of his knowledge and understanding.

One day, however, determined to follow the example of his great ancestor Hachiman Tarō Yoshiie, he resolves to leave the temple when he has reached his fourteenth year to avenge the death of his father. In preparation for this quest, he prays to Bishamon for guidance and receives a divine revelation in a dream. Following the directions he has been given by Bishamon, he makes his way into the depths of the mountains, where he finally comes upon a wall of many colors, the wall of the Great Tengu's palace.

He introduces himself as an acolyte of Kurama-dera, but the Great Tengu is not taken in and recognizes his visitor immediately as Ushiwaka. Delighted, he summons Tarōbō from Mount Atago, Jirōbō from Mount Hira, Saburōbō from Mount Kōya, Shirōbō from Mount Nachi, Hōkōbō from the Tang capital, and even Nichirinbō from India. These adepts of the secret arts of the Tengu demonstrate their magical powers for the awestruck Ushiwaka.

The wife of the Great Tengu is the daughter of a wealthy man in the province of Kai and has a great fondness for human beings. She arranges an encounter with Ushiwaka. During the course of their conversation, she tells Ushiwaka that her husband flies every day to the one hundred and thirty-six Buddhist hells and the Western Paradise. Furthermore, Ushiwaka's father Yoshitomo has been reincarnated as the Buddha Dainichi Nyorai and is now the ruler of the nine paradises, and her husband should be able to take Ushiwaka to visit him. Delighted, Ushiwaka appeals to the Great Tengu, who agrees to escort him.

They set out, passing through the hell of fire, the hell of blood, the hell of starving demons, and Ashuradō, finally arriving in the Pure Land of the Western Paradise. The turrets of countless palaces sparkle with the divine light of the seven jewels, and music of sublime beauty resonates through the air. The Great Tengu bids Ushiwaka wait and begs an audience for him with Yoshitomo. Yoshitomo refuses to grant an audience, however, citing the Buddhist doctrine that the bond between parent and child lasts only one lifetime. The Great Tengu beseeches him to reconsider, and finally he assents.

First, he tests Ushiwaka by asking him a great many questions concerning the Buddhist Law. It is only after Ushiwaka has displayed his profound knowledge that father and son enjoy a tearful reunion. Ushiwaka tells his father that he has resolved to leave the priesthood to seek revenge on the Taira. Delighted, Yoshitomo says, "Very well, I will tell you what lies in your future." The following is the story of Ushiwaka's future, as told to him by his father.

As Hōgan Yoshitsune, he will go to the capital to slay one thousand Taira retainers

on the Gojō Bridge. He will meet a strange priest called Benkei, who will become his most trusted retainer. He will accompany a gold merchant to Ōshū, and on the way he will kill two famous bandits, Sekihara Yoichi and Kumasaka Chōhan. He will fall gravely ill and die at Fukiage no Hama, but will be brought back from the dead by the prayers of a beautiful woman, Lady Jōruri. After visiting Ōshū, he will steal a famous treatise on war from Kiichi Hōgen and will also obtain a secret treatise on war from the demon ruler of the Kiman kingdom. Finally he will join his brother Yoritomo in a great rebellion against the Taira and will defeat them in the Western Sea. However, he will be slandered by Kajiwara no Kagetoki, and Yoritomo will raise a force against him. Surrounded at his Takadachi mansion in Ōshū, he will die by his own hand.

At the end of his story, Yoshitomo warns Ushiwaka that everything depends on one's deeds in previous lives and admonishes him not to neglect his devotions. After permitting him a glimpse of the world of the three thousand Great Oxen, he sends Ushiwaka on his way. Reluctant to part with his father, Ushiwaka nevertheless finds himself back in the palace of the Great Tengu. He begs to be accepted as a disciple of the Great Tengu, and they pledge to be teacher and disciple. Ushiwaka prepares to set off on the return journey to Kurama, but just as he begins his farewell speech he finds himself miraculously back in the chambers of his master, Tōkōbō of Kurama-dera.

Kanei-era edition. Large *orihon* book. One volume. Fifteen illustrations; approximately 19.0 cm by 14.5 cm.

In the same way that many of the *otogizōshi* about Yoshitsune or the Soga brothers are elaborations of episodes in the *noh* tales or related legends, Sagoromo is based very loosely on *Sagoromo Monogatari*, a work of the mid-eleventh century that gains second only to *The Tale of Genji* in the region of classical Japanese literature.

During the long reign of Emperor Kiranei [in *Sagoromo Monogatari*, the emperor is Ichijō (reigned 986–1011)], there is a young Middle Captain named Sagoromo, whose father is the Minister of the Center. He is famous at court for his mastery of the flute, and it is said that the beauty of his music is such as to lure the gods themselves from heaven. He is also famous as a lover, and his fondness for nocturnal adventures often makes him

# Sagoromo さごろも

## The Story of Middle Captain Sagoromo

Kanei-era edition. Large upright book. One volume. Fifteen illustrations, approximately 19.0 cm by 14.5 cm.

*In the same way that many of the* otogizōshi *about Yoshitsune or the Soga brothers are elaborations of episodes in the war tales or related legends,* Sagoromo *is based very loosely on* Sagoromo Monogatari, *a work of the mid-eleventh century that ranks second only to* The Tale of Genji *in the corpus of classical Japanese literature.*

During the long reign of Emperor Kinmei [in *Sagoromo Monogatari*, the emperor is Ichijō (reigned 986–1011)], there is a young Middle Captain named Sagoromo, whose father is the Minister of the Center. He is famous at court for his mastery of the flute, and it is said that the beauty of his music is such as to lure the gods themselves from heaven. He is also famous as a lover, and his fondness for nocturnal adventures often makes him

153

154

the subject of comparisons with the shining Prince Genji. Once, in his nineteenth year, he is returning to the imperial palace from one of his escapades when he has an extraordinary experience that changes his fate completely.

He comes upon the carriage of a lady of high rank and interrupts a monk from Kiyomizudera in the act of attempting to kidnap the lady, who has been in seclusion at Uzumasadera. Sagoromo rescues the lady, and she reveals that her name is Asukai and that she is the daughter of the Middle Councilor who lives at Nishi Dōin in Nijō. Deeply impressed by the lady's beauty, he forgets his other lovers and begins to visit her every night. Soon she confesses that she is carrying his child.

It so happens that Hyōbu no Taifu Michinari, the son of Sagoromo's wet nurse, is appointed commander of Dazaifu, the imperial office in Tsukushi (Kyushu). Before his departure, a certain person suggests that he should marry and promises to find an appropriate candidate. This person approaches the Middle Councilor, who knows nothing of the affair between his daughter and Sagoromo, and he agrees to a match between Asukai and Michinari. Unable to reveal the secret of her pregnancy, Asukai has no choice but to accompany Michinari to Tsukushi.

While they are aboard ship, however, Michinari shows her a fan that he received from Sagoromo as a going-away present. On it are two poems that she had exchanged with Sagoromo, two poems they had written on the fan as a symbol of their pledge of love. Overcome with grief, she attempts to throw herself into the sea at a place called Muronotsu off the coast of the province of Suō. It so happens, however, that the ship of her elder brother, who has become a monk at the temple of Anraku-ji in Tsukushi, is passing by at that very instant on its way to the capital, and Asukai lands on its deck. Her brother rescues her and takes her back to the capital.

When Asukai's elder brother tells their father what has happened, the Middle Councilor is outraged and berates him for his unfilial conduct. Left with no other choice, he takes Asukai away to live in Tokiwa, a place in the western suburbs of the capital.

On the day of Asukai's departure for Tsukushi, Sagoromo steals into her bed chamber as always and is shocked to find that she has disappeared. Repeated inquiries yield nothing as to her whereabouts, so taking along a trusted servant he departs from the capital to search for her. Five years pass in fruitless searching. In the meantime, Asukai bears him a son and the boy enters his fourth year.

Tortured by pity for Asukai, her elder brother resolves to offer prayers to the Great Buddha in Nara. Perhaps because the Great Buddha is aware of his resolve, it so happens that on the day of his visit to Nara he encounters Sagoromo himself, who has despaired of finding Asukai and also resolved to offer prayers to the Great Buddha. Overjoyed, he returns with the monk to Tokiwa and meets his son for the first time.

After only a short time, however, Sagoromo receives word that Asukai has died. Insane with grief, he uncovers her grave and opens her casket. Strangely enough, death has brought no change to her beautiful features. He and his son, who has accompanied Sagoromo to the grave, offer agonized prayers to all the gods and Buddhas. Their prayers are answered, and Asukai is suddenly restored to life.

The Minister of the Center, Sagoromo's father, is overjoyed to learn from his son's servant that Sagoromo is alive and has returned safely to the capital. He goes to Tokiwa himself to bring Sagoromo, Lady Asukai, and Sagoromo's son back to the palace. The emperor is also pleased with these developments, and Sagoromo is given a high court rank and succeeds his father as the Minister of the Center. Asukai's elder brother is awarded with the position of high priest of the Tendai Buddhist sect.

# Onzōshi Shima-watari 御曹司島渡

## Yoshitsune's Voyage to Fabulous Islands

Meireki-era (1655–58) edition. Oblong book. One volume extant of an original two-volume set. Eight illustrations, approximately 13.5 cm by 21.5 cm.

Minamoto no Yoshitsune leaves Kurama-dera with a gold merchant bound for Fujiwara no Hidehira's capital in Ōshū, in the hope that he can form an alliance with Hidehira against the Taira. He is welcomed by Hidehira, who promises to aid Yoshitsune in his quest. One day, Hidehira tells Yoshitsune about the fabulous island of Chishima in the northern sea, where the great demon king Kanehira has established a magnificent capital called Kikenjō. This Kanehira has in his possession a scroll bearing a magical military treatise entitled *Dainichi no Hō*. Hidehira advises Yoshitsune that if he can obtain this treatise he will be able to carry out his plan for winning mastery of Japan.

Yoshitsune travels to the port of Tosa on the Tsugaru Straits, where he purchases a great ship called *Hayakaze* (*Swift Wind*) and then sets off in search of Chishima in the seas beyond Ezo (Hokkaido). On the prow of the ship, he erects an image of the Daihitamon-ten of Kurama-dera, and on its stern an image of Hachiman, the guardian deity of the Minamoto. He fills the ship with gods and Buddhas and, calling on them for divine guidance, allows the wind to take the ship where it will.

He passes many strange islands and, on the seventy-fifth day, finally reaches the island of Kiyōgarugajima, where the inhabitants are one hundred feet tall and have equine heads and trunks but human legs. Another eighty days of sailing brings him to Hadakajima, where the inhabitants are completely naked because they do not know how to make cloth. There, he uses his magic powers to summon eighty bolts of fine linen from Echigo. Setting sail again, he travels seventy-six days before reaching an island called Nyōgo no Shima. There are no men on the island, and the female inhabitants propose to kill him in order to make his spirit their guardian deity. He escapes with his life by charming the women with the magical music of his flute, Taitōmaru. Finally, at the island of Ezonojima, he learns how to find Kanehira's capital on Chishima.

Long months and years have passed, but Yoshitsune finally reaches the fabulous island of Chishima. As he approaches the palace of the great demon Kanehira, he is surrounded by hundreds of demons, who prepare to kill him. As he has done in countless dangerous situations during the voyage, he persuades them to spare his life by playing for them on his flute. He is taken to Kanehira, who is enchanted by his playing and finally in a friendly manner asks him his purpose in coming to Kikenjō. Yoshitsune explains that he has studied the magical martial arts of the Tengu as a disciple of the great Tengu adept Tarōbō at Kurama-dera, and that now he wishes to learn the secrets of the *Dainichi no Hō*. Kanehira accepts Yoshitsune as his disciple and teaches him many secrets of magical martial arts, but he refuses to instruct him in the *Dainichi no Hō*.

Kanehira stages a great banquet, ordering Yoshitsune to play for him once again. It is at this banquet that Yoshitsune first encounters Princess Asahi, Kanehira's human daughter. Yoshitsune falls deeply in love with her at first sight, and, after stealing into her chambers several times, he is finally successful in winning her. One day, after they

have been lovers for some time, Yoshitsune tells her of his wish to see the *Dainichi no Hō* and begs her to help him. Princess Asahi, herself deeply in love with Yoshitsune, braves many perils to travel far into the mountains where the scroll has been hidden. She finally manages to find the scroll and bring it back to Kikenjō, where Yoshitsune works for three days and three nights without rest to copy it. When he has finished, he is amazed to find that the writing in the original scroll has completely disappeared.

Terrified, Princess Asahi urges Yoshitsune to flee before the theft of the scroll is discovered. Yoshitsune's escape is followed by many strange occurrences, revealing to Kanehira that the scroll has been stolen. Kanehira is enraged and dispatches one thousand Ahōrasetsu devils to capture Yoshitsune. Yoshitsune uses magical arts of war revealed to him by Princess Asahi to escape his pursuers. When first they draw near, he uses the "art of the salt mountain" to raise a huge mountain of salt from the sea, blocking his attackers. Finally he uses the "art of swift wind," which returns him instantly to the harbor of Tosa in Japan.

Insane with anger, Kanehira attacks Princess Asahi and tears her into eight pieces. In fact, however, Princess Asahi is a manifestation of the Benzai-ten of Enoshima in Japan, who pitied Yoshitsune and was born as the human daughter of the great demon king Kanehira in order to aid Yoshitsune in his quest to restore the Minamoto family to power. Yoshitsune, who has returned to Hidehira's capital in Ōshū, learns of Lady Asahi's death in a miraculous dream. Lady Asahi appears and instructs him to perform the art of *Nurete no Hō*. He writes two magical characters, and a drop of blood appears on the paper, a sign that his lover has died. Stricken with grief, he arranges to have memorial services performed for her in temples all over the country.

Manjūrō (1655–58) edition. Oblong book. One volume. Five illustrations, approximately 13.0 cm by 22.5 cm.

This is one of the many legends dealing with the lives of famous court poets. Izumi Shikibu, though she has certainly not a courtesan, was famous for her many unhappy love affairs and even sexually explicit poetry.

During the rule of ex-Emperor Ichijō, there is a courtesan called Izumi Shikibu, who has her first love affair at the age of twelve with Tachibana no Yasumasa. The following year, she gives birth to a male child and, fearful that she will become the object of cruel gossip, abandons the infant on the Gojō Bridge. She writes a poem on the inside of the collar of his kimono and lays a small dagger by his side. She keeps the sheath as a remembrance of the child and leaves him.

The child is found by a townsman, who takes him home and cares for him. When he reaches the appropriate age, his adopted father sends him to Mount Hiei to become a priest. By the time he has reached adulthood, he is known far and wide as a monk of unparalleled wisdom. Indeed, he is given the name of a Buddhist saint, Dōmei Ajari. In his seventeenth year, he is summoned to the emperor's private chambers to perform a reading of the Lotus Sutra. As he is chanting, a gust of wind suddenly lifts the screen concealing the emperor's ladies-in-waiting. He catches a glimpse of a beautiful woman of about thirty years and instantly falls in love. This lady's his mother, Izumi Shikibu. Dōmei returns to Mount Hiei but finds himself unable to forget the lady he has glimpsed

# Izumi Shikibu 和泉式部

## The Story of Izumi Shikibu

Meireki-era (1655–58) edition. Oblong book. One volume. Five illustrations, approximately 13.0 cm by 22.5 cm.

*This is one of the many legends dealing with the lives of famous court poets. Izumi Shikibu, though she was certainly not a courtesan, was famous for her many unhappy love affairs and often sexually explicit poetry.*

During the rule of ex-Emperor Ichijō, there is a courtesan called Izumi Shikibu, who has her first love affair at the age of twelve with Tachibana no Yasumasa. The following year, she gives birth to a male child and, fearful that she will become the subject of cruel gossip, abandons the infant on the Gojō Bridge. She writes a poem on the inside of the collar of his kimono and lays a small dagger by his side. She keeps the sheath as a remembrance of the child and leaves him.

The child is found by a townsman, who takes him home and cares for him. When he reaches the appropriate age, his adopted father sends him to Mount Hiei to become a priest. By the time he has reached adulthood, he is known far and wide as a monk of unparalleled wisdom. Indeed, he is given the name of a Buddhist saint, Dōmei Ajari.

In his seventeenth year, he is summoned to the emperor's private chambers to perform a reading of the Lotus Sutra. As he is chanting, a gust of wind suddenly lifts the screen concealing the emperor's ladies-in-waiting. He catches a glimpse of a beautiful woman of about thirty years and instantly falls in love. This lady is his mother, Izumi Shikibu.

Dōmei returns to Mount Hiei but finds himself unable to forget the lady he has glimpsed

behind the screen. He goes to the capital again and, disguising himself as a mandarin orange peddler, manages to gain entrance to the emperor's ladies' quarters. As he is selling oranges to the ladies-in-waiting, a servant girl emerges from Izumi Shikibu's room. She gives Dōmei twenty pennies and asks for twenty oranges. Dōmei begins counting out the oranges but composes a witty counting poem as he does so, elegantly playing on the references to love in the imperial anthologies of verse. The servant finds this strange indeed and questions him. He replies evasively, saying "Falling, falling."

The servant relates this incident to her mistress, who commands her to follow Dōmei and find out where his lodgings are. Izumi Shikibu has recognized Dōmei's allusion to a famous poem sent by Lady Ise to the shining Prince Genji:

| 君恋ふる | Lost in thoughts of you |
|---|---|
| 涙の雨に | My sleeves are soaked by |
| 袖ぬれて | A rain of tears. |
| ほさんとすれば | Even as I try to dry them, |
| 又はふりふり | Again, falling, falling. |

Deeply impressed by the wit and refinement displayed in this illusion, she bids her servant take her to Dōmei's lodgings, where she composes the following poem:

| 出でてほせ | Come out and dry them |
|---|---|
| 今宵ばかりの | Under the moon that |
| 月かげに | Shines only for tonight, |
| ふりふり濡らす | Your sleeves soaked with |
| 恋の袂を | A rain of tears, falling, falling. |

Feeling as if he were in a dream, Dōmei composes the following poem:

behind the screen. He goes to the capital again and, disguising himself as a mandarin-orange peddler, manages to gain entrance to the emperor's ladies' quarters. As he is selling oranges to the ladies-in-waiting, a servant girl emerges from Izumi Shikibu's room. She gives Domei twenty pennies and asks for twenty oranges. Domei begins counting out the oranges but composes a witty counting poem as he does so, elegantly playing on the references to love in the imperial anthologies of verse. The servant finds this strange indeed and questions him. He replies evasively, saying, "Falling, falling, falling".

The servant relates this incident to her mistress, who commands her to follow Domei and find out where his lodgings are. Izumi Shikibu has recognized Domei's allusion to a famous poem sent by Lady Ise to the shining Prince Genji:

> Lost in thoughts of you
> ... soaked by
> ...
> Even as I try to dry them,
> Again, falling, falling.

Deeply impressed by the wit and refinement displayed in this illusion, she bids her servant take her to Domei's lodgings, where she composes the following poem:

> Come out and dry them
> Under the moon that
> Shines only for tonight,
> Your sleeves soaked with
> A rain of tears, falling, falling.

Feeling as if he were in a dream, Domei composes the following poem:

　　　　　　　　　　　　Though I do not come out,

　　　　　　　　　　　　If you have a heart,

　　　　　　　　　　　　Lend me your radiance,

　　　　　　　　　　　　Like the moon at dawn,

　　　　　　　　　　　　Illuminate the darkness.

The lady enters, and they pass the night in an embrace of love. As dawn begins to break, the lady catches sight of a small unsheathed dagger in Dōmei's room. She asks him where he got it. He explains that he was abandoned on Gojō Bridge as an infant, and that the dagger had been found beside him. She questions him further, and he tells her that he was found wearing a kimono, on the collar of which someone had written a poem. He recites the poem, and she recognizes it as the one she had written herself seventeen years before. She shows him the sheath of the dagger, which she has kept near her heart for all these years, and collapses in tears, thinking that it is only in this world of sorrow that a mother could have an affair with her own child without recognizing him.

She leaves the capital and enters the temple of Mount Shosha in the province of Harima, where she becomes the disciple of Shōkū Shōnin, a great Buddhist sage. She achieves satori in her sixtieth year and inscribes the following poem on the central pillar of the temple:

　　　　　　　　　　　　From a world of darkness

　　　　　　　　　　　　Into a world of darkness

　　　　　　　　　　　　We are born.

　　　　　　　　　　　　O moon, rising from the mountain,

　　　　　　　　　　　　Shine brightly through the darkness.

　　　　It is said that the term "poem pillar" originated in this incident.

| 出でずとも | Though I do not come out, |
| 心のあらば | If you have a heart, |
| 影さして | Lend me your radiance. |
| 闇をば照らせ | Like the moon at dawn, |
| 有明の月 | Illuminate the darkness. |

The lady enters, and they pass the night in an embrace of love. As dawn begins to break, the lady catches sight of a small unsheathed dagger in Dōmei's room. She asks him where he got it. He explains that he was abandoned on Gojō Bridge as an infant, and that the dagger had been found beside him. She questions him further, and he tells her that he was found wearing a kimono, on the collar of which someone had written a poem. He recites the poem, and she recognizes it as the one she had written herself seventeen years before. She shows him the sheath of the dagger, which she has kept near her heart for all these years, and collapses in tears, thinking that it is only in this world of sorrow that a mother could have an affair with her own child without recognizing him.

She leaves the capital and enters the temple of Mount Shosha in the province of Harima, where she becomes the disciple of Shōkū Shōnin, a great Buddhist sage. She achieves *satori* in her sixtieth year and inscribes the following poem on the central pillar of the temple:

| 暗きより | From a world of darkness |
| 暗き闇路に | Into a world of darkness |
| 生れきて | We are born. |
| さやかに照らせ | O moon, rising from the mountain, |
| 山の端の月 | Shine brightly through the darkness. |

It is said that the term "poem pillar" originated in this incident.

# *Hachikazuki*
鉢 かづき

## The Story of Lady Hachikazuki

Kanei-era old movable wooden type edition. Large upright book. One volume (some leaves missing). Six illustrations, approximately 20.1 cm by 13.9 cm. (For a complete translation, see Chigusa Stevens, "Hachikazuki: A Muromachi Short Story," *Monumenta Nipponica*, vol. 32, no. 3, Autumn 1977).

Sanetaka, the governor of Bitchū, lives in the city of Katano, the provincial capital. He is fabulously wealthy and there is nothing to spoil his happiness except the fact that he and his beloved wife are childless. Despite their advanced age, however, his wife at last bears him a baby girl. Overjoyed, the couple make a pilgrimage to the temple of Hasedera and offer prayers to Kannon to protect the child and to bring her a happy future.

When the young lady is in her twelfth year, her mother falls grievously ill. She summons her daughter and places a heavy box on her head, covering it with a large bowl that comes down to the girl's shoulders, hiding her face. Without explaining this strange act, she recites the following poem:

| | |
|---|---|
| さしも草 | O Kannon, |
| 深くぞ頼む | As a living creature, |
| 観世音 | My faith in you is deep. |
| 誓のままに | As I have pledged, |
| いただかせぬる | I make her wear this bowl. |

After intoning the poem, she dies. Sanetaka tries to remove the bowl, but it is stuck too tightly. Mourning her mother's death and her own plight at having become a weird and freakish creature, the young lady passes many long and unhappy days and months, and people begin calling her Hachikazuki (the princess who wears a bowl). Finally her father remarries, and Hachikazuki's stepmother takes an instant dislike to her. She slanders Hachikazuki to her father, and her father, completely taken in, abandons her in the wilderness.

In despair, Hachikazuki throws herself into a large river, but the bowl keeps her afloat, and she is finally rescued by fishermen. She is wandering about in a daze, not knowing where she is, when she is spotted by Middle Captain Yamakage, the governor of the province. He takes pity on her and puts her to work tending the fire in his bathhouse. The people in his mansion ridicule her mercilessly, and once again she sinks into despair. One day, however, the governor's fourth son, Onzōshi Saishō, catches a glimpse of Hachikazuki when he goes for a bath late in the evening. Deeply moved by the beauty of her hands and feet, he woos her, and they spend the night together. Hearing rumors that Saishō is visiting Hachikazuki every night, his mother sends his old wet nurse to admonish him against associating with such a strange creature. Saishō ignores his mother's pleas and becomes even more brazen in his pursuit of Hachikazuki, stealing into her bedchamber morning and night.

Fearful that her son has become too involved with Hachikazuki, his mother schemes

with his old wet nurse to drive her away. They hit upon the scheme of having a beauty contest among all of the wives of the four sons, hoping that Hachikazuki will be too embarrassed to appear and will leave. As they have planned, Hachikazuki resolves to leave as soon as she hears of the contest. However, Saishō insists that he will leave with her. As they tearfully prepare to run away together, they exchange sad poems. Suddenly the bowl breaks and falls away, revealing Hachikazuki's incomparably beautiful countenance. In the box on her head, Saishō finds beautiful kimono and jewelry. Hachikazuki dons layers and layers of kimono, and prepares the remaining treasures as presents for the governor and his wife.

The wives of Saishō's brothers are stunned by the appearance of this unparalleled beauty and by the splendid array of gifts she has brought. However, they quickly collect their wits and, suggesting that beautiful as she is Hachikazuki is no doubt of low birth and quite unrefined, insist that she submit to a number of tests. She plays the Japanese lute, composes poetry, and demonstrates her mastery of calligraphy, displaying a background of exquisite elegance. The governor and his wife gasp with amazement, and the governor celebrates his son's discovery of this unrivaled jewel by granting him the lion's share of his domain.

In the meantime, Sanetaka has fallen out with Hachikazuki's stepmother and has left behind his riches to become a wandering ascetic. Regretting his treatment of his daughter, he makes a pilgrimage to Hase-dera and entreats Kannon to allow him to meet her once more. It so happens that Saishō is also on a pilgrimage to Hase-dera to celebrate his appointment as governor of the provinces of Yamato, Kawachi, and Iga. They meet, and Sanetaka's wish for a reunion with his daughter is fulfilled. Overjoyed to learn the true identity of his bride, Saishō relinquishes the province of Kawachi to Sanetaka and makes Sanetaka's son his heir. Thus the sad story of Hachikazuki has a very happy ending indeed.

# Shishō no Uta-awase 四生の歌合

## The Poetry Contests of the Four Living Things

Kanei-era old movable wooden type edition. Large upright book. Two volumes. Fifty-seven illustrations, approximately 27.7 cm by 18.0 cm. Volume one is in the collection of the Tōyō Bunko.

On the night of the first full moon in the tenth month, a great crowd of crawling creatures is assembled in a garden. After a while, the cricket faces the others and makes a speech. "It is the time of the year when one always tends to feels lonely. Let us bare our hearts under this beautiful moon and take turns composing elegant poems." The other crawling creatures agree, and each finds a fallen leaf upon which to assume the appropriate posture for intoning his composition. The toad, who lives in the bushes nearby, joins the gathering and suggests that they make it a contest. Everyone agrees enthusiastically to this splendid proposal, and they promptly appoint the toad to act as judge. Then they pair off. The cricket is paired with the bee, the millipede with the ant, the grasshopper with the bagworm, the praying mantis with the wire worm, the green caterpillar with

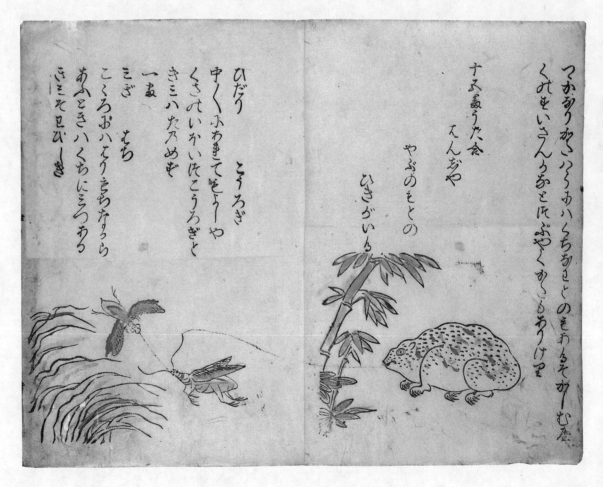

左　くも

えくゐさよいをバ人に
なぐさどそこがあふせにハ
うらないそあし

十四番

右　せミ

なさけなくかくここころハ
なかしやせミのなかしよ
男をやなけなん

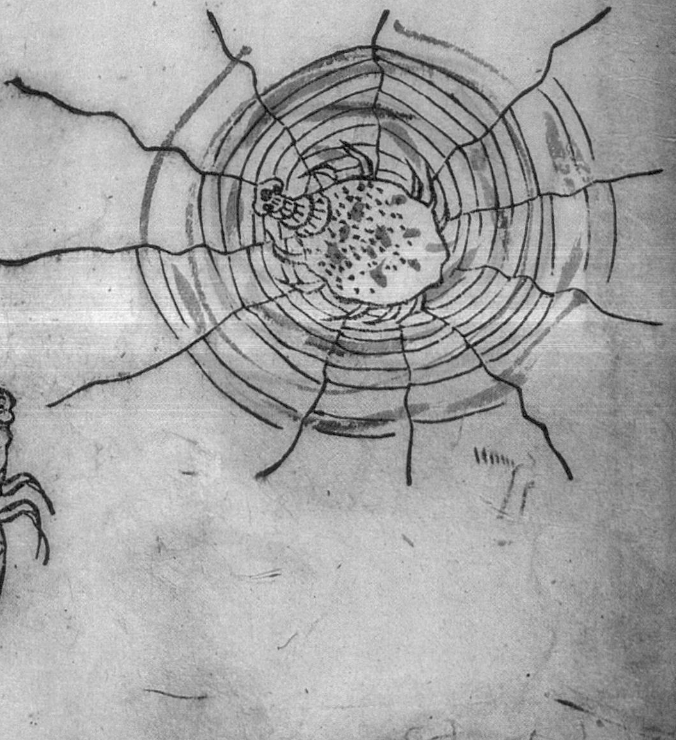

たのきとれ三そさい
きうこつやいくさばうそを
はきうまにうく我をきけを
さそます

十あざいゆうみふける恋

右にかをづら乃こうもうと
わて心でにさこうも里と
みせあさん志かをほらして

ふよりをとらんに重しき

the butterfly, the hairy caterpillar with the giant katydid, the little katydid with the earth-worm, the bell-ring bug with the pine cricket, the centipede with the termite, the evening cicada with the golden bug, the fly with the mosquito, the flea with the louse, the mole cricket with the firefly, and the spider with the locust. Thus, they stage a poetry contest in fourteen rounds. In fact, they had planned to make it fifteen rounds, with the toad against the snake in the fifteenth. When the time comes for him to make a judgment on his round with the snake, however, the toad becomes frightened. Completely nonplused he is unable to award a decision and runs away to hide under some fallen leaves in the bamboo glade.

One day in the spring rainy season, the wren who lives under the eaves makes a visit to his friend Chikurinbō the bush warbler. He tells Chikurinbō about the poetry contest held by the crawling creatures. It is well known that the birds belong to the Minamoto family, the crawling creatures to the Taira family, the beasts to the Fujiwara family, and the water creatures to the Tachibana family. They agree that it would be an intolerable loss of face to leave unchallenged the famous poetry contest of the crawling creatures. Fortunately, there is a certain lady, by the name of Usohime, who has attracted a good deal of attention from all the male birds, so they are in an excellent position to organize a poetry contest on the topic of love.

Chikurinbō points out that they cannot very well organize such an important event without consulting the eagle, the king of the birds. The wren agrees, and they send Dō-saibō the owl as a messenger to the eagle. The eagle thinks it a splendid idea and dispatches the wren and the bush warbler as emissaries to the water creatures and the beasts,

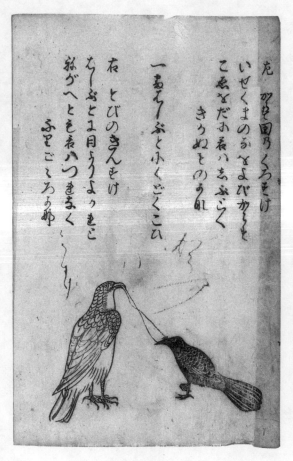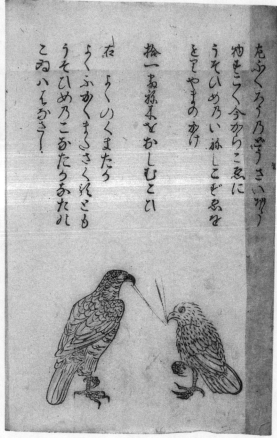

左あまうあざぬかりの行く

山のいもふちせふかとる

あをだかとうきことゝなりて

　　　をゝりをらん

口蓋

右　あまぞのひよん太郎

風乃ふくゆさき乃たきる

たさる魚かるあまつらさげて

こかきゆくふ孫

suggesting that they organize poetry contests as well. The eagle appoints himself as the judge of the contest and pairs off the birds for a fifteen-round poetry contest. The black-eared kite is paired off with the crow, the copper pheasant with the ring-necked pheasant, the top tit with the great tit, the sparrow with the red meadow bunting, the cuckoo with the bush warbler, the swallow with the robin, the white-cheeked meadow bunting with the coal tit, the long-tailed rose-finch with the greenfinch, the chicken with the duck, the wren with the bat, the owl with the crested eagle, the peewee with the water-rail, the Mandarin duck with the gull, the dove with the gray starling, and the plover with the jay.

After the birds stage their contest, they collaborate with the crawling creatures to compile a collection of the poems from the two contests.

The poems from the poetry contests arranged by the water creatures and the beasts are collected in volume two of this edition, but no account of the circumstances of the contests is given. A glance at the illustrations will reveal the way the water creatures and the beasts were paired off.

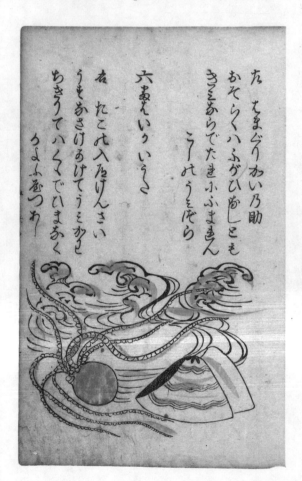

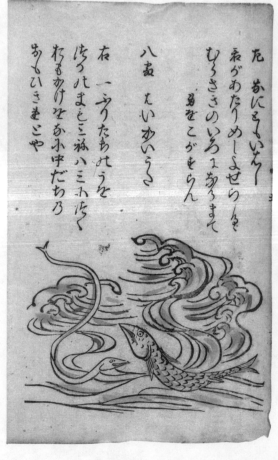

たりうひけのゑびへをん

ゑぢがたくひひかりこをえよ
かく斗うきゑにそへて
たゑぬたゑひを

九ゑありゆのうこ

右　あにうにおをひの助
からころをに一きのそてを
かくしゆうた孫小たに
たのむおをうけ

173

た　いぬ山れに郎太

いつそりたつきえるまぬ

れもかけやまかに八又せぬ

月そりおーき

二書月小まちふりをひ

た　さる丸のりうだ少ふ

ふまちやたちてそねてそ

をち月の衫もかけ八いさ

よひふりをまて

174

左　い乃ちをしらん
くミて志乃なさけハいかほ
いかり井のゐいにこそふかく
心こそさま

三　妻あハでなかすこひ

右　山乃ゐの志ゝ乃助
流まとゑるをなゐをかいて
さをしか乃なくこゑさへぞ
うらやまれぬる

たこ ふうこられをけ
きらハまて刕ハから竹の
中となり ふうぶつせ丹そ
いけりかとく

九當おぢら松く 患

右 珎山大かめ
祢れしさやいくたび人を
大のめ乃珎ちに目くまて
 うよふもそうき

# *Kanazōshi*

## 仮名草子

# Usuyuki Monogatari     薄雪物語

## The Tale of Lady Usuyuki

Kanei 9 (1632) edition. Large upright book. Two volumes. Ten illustrations, approximately 19.5 cm by 15.0 cm.

*Usuyuki Monogatari is a highly unusual example of the genre of* kanazōshi. *It displays little of the elaborate narrative structure of* The Tale of Genji *or later examples of classical tale literature, but resembles much more closely older works such as* Yamato Monogatari *(A Tale of Yamato). The emphasis on poetry in* Usuyuki Monogatari *suggests a new development in early Edo-period literature. While the story was undoubtedly read for entertainment, it is likely that it was also used as a text for studying classical styles of poetry.*

In the village of Fukakusa near the capital, there lives a man of extraordinarily effeminate demeanor named Sonobe no Emon. One day, he sets off on a pilgrimage to Kiyomizu-dera. As he enters the temple grounds he comes upon a palanquin out of which palanquin emerges a lady of such great beauty that he can think of no one to compare her to but the famous beauties of the past. Visions of Yang Guifei, Madame Li, Ono no Komachi, and Lady Sannomiya dance through his head. Already helplessly in love, he purifies himself at the Otonashi waterfall and appears before the Kiyomizu Kannon, beseeching the deity for assistance in winning the lady's heart. Perhaps because Kannon has heard his impas-

sioned prayers, he encounters the lady's servant, who happens to pass by at just that moment, and feigning only casual interest contrives to ask her the name of her mistress. He learns that the lady is called Lady Usuyuki and that she is the sixteen-year-old daughter of Saisaki Izumi, who serves in the ladies' quarters of the Ichijō Palace.

Having discovered the lady's identity, Sonobe no Emon becomes even more determined to make her his own and begs the servant to act as his messenger. She agrees, and he leans against a tree to compose a love poem. Folding the paper in a charming manner, he gives the poem to the servant, who carries it to her mistress. Things continue for some time in this manner, and each time Sonobe no Emon sends a message the lady responds with an elegant reply, stubbornly refusing to accept his advances. Though he quotes the famous love stories of China and Japan, pours his heart into beautiful poems of love in the classical style, the lady insists that, as a married woman, it would be inappropriate to carry the affair further and cites her own famous examples of loyal wives.

After they have exchanged messages twelve times, Sonobe no Emon sends this poem:

| | |
|---|---|
| たづねかね | Difficult to follow, |
| 知らぬ山路を | The unknown mountain path. |
| まよふ身に | To one who has lost his way, |
| 君がありかを | Make known your whereabouts, |
| そこと知らせよ | My Lady. |

To this, the lady replies simply, "The thin snow [*usuyuki*] in the valley's shade is not something of this life." (In Japanese, the word for "life" is homophonous with "night.")

Sonobe no Emon is heartbroken, interpreting the poem to mean that the lady intends to refuse him forever in this life. Someone suggests to him, however, that the lady has alluded to this famous old poem from an imperial anthology:

| | |
|---|---|
| 谷蔭に | Even the thin snow |
| 降るうす雪も | That falls |
| 春日にて | In the valley's shadow |
| 人知れずこそ | Melts on a spring day, |
| とくるものかな | Though people are unaware. |

In fact, says Sonobe no Emon's friend, the lady is suggesting that, while it might be impossible tonight, she has resolved to give him her love tomorrow. His grief completely forgotten, Sonobe no Emon sends Lady Usuyuki a poem that delicately reveals his understanding of her message and begs her to admit him to her chambers that very evening. Late that night, he steals into the lady's bed chamber, and the bond of love is sealed.

Their affair continues for nearly a year, but Sonobe no Emon is suddenly called away to the village of Shiga in the province of Ōmi, where a relative has fallen gravely ill. He is detained in Shiga for over a month, and in the meantime Lady Usuyuki falls ill and, despite the frantic ministrations of her parents, dies. When Sonobe no Emon hears of her death on his return from Shiga, he becomes insane with grief and resolves to commit suicide and join the lady in paradise. Finally, however, he reconsiders and, changing his name to Renshō Hōshi, travels to Mount Kōya to practice religious austerities. Later, he returns to the capital and builds a grass hut near a temple on Higashiyama, where he devotes his time to prayers for Lady Usuyuki. In his twenty-fifth year, he achieves enlightenment and dies.

Kan'ei 12 (1635) edition. Large upright book. One volume of two extant. Eleven illustrations; approximately 19.5 cm by 13.0 cm.

*Shichinin Bikuni is an excellent source of information concerning wandering nuns, or bikuni, who played a central role in the development of oral literature in medieval Japan. The stories of personal suffering caused by the nuns in this kanazōshi are also superficial examples of one of the major genres of storytelling practiced by wandering nuns, the setsuwa, or the telling of beyond concerning Buddhist morality tales or Buddhist deities (honji).*

Near a river called Sekikawa in the province of Shinano, two mendicant nuns called Ko-Amidabutsu (Old Amida Buddha) and Kon-Amidabutsu (New Amida Buddha) open a public bath, at which they offer bathing facilities and lodgings to travelers passing by. One day near the end of the ninth month, five other mendicant nuns stop for the night there, and the seven nuns pass the long autumn night relating the stories of personal suffering that led them to leave the world and find salvation in religion.

The first to tell her story had been a courtesan in the capital by the name of Shiragiku. She had fallen in love, but her lover had returned to his home province. Another man had made advances, and they had become intimate. Eventually he had taken her back with him to his own province of Mino. Her new husband was so kind to her that she became the object of envy among the other women in the village; but she herself had found it impossible to forget her former lover. When she was informed of his death, she had run away to become a nun.

The second nun had been the wife of a certain saikyō, who lived in the Jōhōji district of the capital. They had been very happy until one day, through a careless mistake, her husband had caused the death of their three-year-old son. In deep remorse, Saikyō had committed suicide, and she had thought to join him and their son in the next world. On the verge of committing suicide herself, she had been persuaded by a certain person to become a nun and spend her life praying for the salvation of her loved ones.

The third nun had been called Hagakusara and had been the daughter of a high-ranking warrior in the ex-emperor's personal guard. She had had a long affair with a warrior from the province of Omi whose name was Okuyama. When his lord was appointed as the emperor's deputy at the Dazaifu in Tsukushi (Kyushu), Okuyama had followed this master, and the two lovers had been forced to part. The following year, Okuyama had sent emissaries to escort her to Tsukushi. Just when she had thought that finally they could be happy, there had been a brief war, and Okuyama had been killed. Heart-broken, she had become a wandering nun.

The fourth nun had been called Hōbu no Kara and, despite the fact that she had been married, had always had a strong desire to leave the world and become a wandering nun. Her preoccupation with Buddhist devotions had led her to neglect her marriage, and indeed, she had had nothing to say to her husband but to press him to awaken to the teachings of Buddhism. Her husband had labored in vain to change her feelings; but finally he himself had achieved enlightenment and had renounced the world. He had become

# Shichinin Bikuni 七人比丘尼

## Seven Mendicant Nuns

Kanei 12 (1635) edition. Large upright book. One volume of two extant. Eleven illustrations, approximately 19.5 cm by 15.0 cm.

*Shichinin Bikuni is an excellent source of information concerning wandering nuns, or* bikuni, *who played a central role in the development of oral literature in medieval Japan. The stories of personal suffering (*zange*) related by the nuns in this* kanazōshi *are also wonderful examples of one of the major themes of the kind of evangelizing practiced by wandering nuns, the other being the telling of legends concerning famous temples or Buddhist deities (*honji*).*

Near a river called Sekigawa in the province of Shinano, two mendicant nuns called Ko-Amidabutsu (Old Amida Buddha) and Kon-Amidabutsu (New Amida Buddha) open a public bath, at which they offer bathing facilities and lodgings to travelers passing by. One day near the end of the ninth month, five other mendicant nuns stop for the night there, and the seven nuns pass the long autumn night relating the stories of personal suffering that led them to leave the world and find salvation in religion.

The first to tell her story had been a courtesan in the capital by the name of Shiragiku. She had fallen in love, but her lover had returned to his home province. Another man had made advances, and they had become intimate. Eventually he had taken her back with him to his own province of Mino. Her new husband was so kind to her that she became the object of envy among the other women in the village, but she herself had found it impossible to forget her former lover. When she was informed of his death, she had run away to become a nun.

The second nun had been the wife of a certain Sakyō, who lived in the Ichijō district of the capital. They had been very happy until one day, through a careless mistake, her husband had caused the death of their three-year-old son. In deep remorse, Sakyō had committed suicide, and she had thought to join him and their son in the next world. On the verge of committing suicide herself, she had been persuaded by a certain person to become a nun and spend her life praying for the salvation of her loved ones.

The third nun had been called Hanakazura and had been the daughter of a high-ranking warrior in the ex-emperor's personal guard. She had had a long affair with a warrior from the province of Ōmi whose name was Okuyama. When his lord was appointed as the emperor's deputy at the Dazaifu in Tsukushi (Kyushu), Okuyama had followed his master, and the two lovers had been forced to part. The following year, Okuyama had sent emissaries to escort her to Tsukushi. Just when she had thought that finally they could be happy, there had been a civil war, and Okuyama had been killed. Heartbroken, she had become a wandering nun.

The fourth nun had been called Hyōbu no Kata and, despite the fact that she had been married, had always had a strong desire to leave the world and become a wandering nun. Her preoccupation with Buddhist devotions had led her to neglect her marriage, and, indeed, she had had nothing to say to her husband but to press him to awaken to the teachings of Buddhism. Her husband had labored in vain to change her feelings, but finally he himself had achieved enlightenment and had renounced the world. He had become a wandering ascetic, and she had soon lost track of him. Free from her marriage, she too had become a wandering nun, and finally her lifelong wish had been fulfilled.

The fifth nun had been the wife of a certain Kikui Ukon of the province of Awa. Her husband had traveled to Kyoto on business of some sort and had returned in the company of a woman with whom he had become intimate in Kyoto. After his return with this woman, she had been shunned and, in her angry jealousy, had been on the verge of being transformed into a snake. One day, however, she had encountered a priest who was passing through their village, and his gentle remonstrances had made her hatred disappear completely. She had become his disciple and had joined the priest in his wanderings.

The sixth nun is Ko-Amidabutsu herself. Before renouncing the world, she had been in the service of the consort of Lord Miike of the province of Chikugo. In addition to his own domain of Chikugo, Lord Miike had won the province of Echigo as the result of a lawsuit. He had traveled to his new domain and there had fallen in love with a certain woman. He had married this woman and had remained in the capital of Echigo. Ko-Amidabutsu had accompanied her mistress to Echigo, where they had pleaded with Lord Miike to reconsider. Slandered by his new wife, they had been driven away without an audience. In despair, her mistress had thrown herself in a river and died. Informed of his principle consort's suicide, Lord Miike had sunk into deep despair and, leaving his domains to his young son, had renounced the world. Ko-Amidabutsu had followed his example and, after long years of austerities at the temple of Zenkō-ji, had wandered around Shinano and finally had established this public bath for travelers.

The last nun to speak is Kon-Amidabutsu. She exclaims that the personal suffering of the others has been quite shallow and, after expounding the deeper principles of the Buddhist Law, leaves the lodging to resume her wanderings. The others press Ko-Amidabutsu to tell the story of Kon-Amidabutsu, and she assents. Kon-Amidabutsu had been the daughter of Hayama no In. At the age of fifteen she had had a love affair with a temple page called Hanawaka, and they had fled the capital to seek refuge in Naniwa (Osaka). The master of their lodgings, unable to control his lust for the lady, had tricked Hanawaka and had murdered him by drowning him in the sea. He had then made advances to the lady, and finally she had been forced to stab him to death. Brokenhearted and full of remorse for having taken human life, she had become a wandering nun.

# Uraminosuke 恨の介

## The Story of Uraminosuke

Kanei-era edition. Large upright book. One volume extant of an original two-volume edition. Five illustrations, approximately 19.0 cm by 14.1 cm.

During the Keichō era (1596–1615), there lives in the capital a young man so famous for his handsome demeanor and his love of erotic adventure that he is often compared to the shining Prince Genji himself. His name is Kuzu no Uraminosuke. On the tenth day of the sixth month of the ninth year of Keichō (1604), there is a lantern festival at Kiyomizu-dera, and Uraminosuke attends with his favorite companions in the ways of love, Omoinosuke, Koinosuke, Midorinosuke, and Ukiyonosuke. When they arrive at the festival, they go their separate ways, and Uraminosuke finds himself at the Tamura Shrine of the temple. He hears someone playing the *koto* with great skill, and discovers that a group of people of high rank are holding a banquet within. Among them is the *koto* player, a lady of fourteen or fifteen years whose beauty can be compared only to that of the famous ladies of the past.

Overcome with passionate thoughts of love, Uraminosuke contrives to follow the lady and spies her entering the Konoe mansion. He returns to his lodgings, but unable to forget the lady he returns to Kiyomizu-dera. After purifying himself, he appears before Kannon and secludes himself in the inner temple chamber for forty-seven days and nights, beseeching Kannon for divine assistance. At dawn on the forty-seventh day, he has a wonderful dream in which Kannon gives him a scroll instructing him to inquire after the lady to the widow of Hattori Shōji, who lives in Ono no Kōji off Matsubara-dōri in Shimogyō. Following the deity's instructions, he makes his way to the widow's mansion and, after being admitted, relates the story of his encounter with the lady, his long seclusion at Kiyomizu-dera, and his strange dream. Hattori Shōji's widow tells him that she has also had a strange dream, and that Kannon has instructed her to reveal to him the lady's identity.

She begins her story by telling him of the death of Toyotomi no Hidetsugu, who had been forced to commit suicide on Mount Kōya by his brother Hideyoshi. Just as Minamoto no Yoritomo had turned against his brother Yoshitsune because of the slanderous insinuations of Kajiwara no Kagetoki, Hideyoshi had forced Hidetsugu to commit suicide because of the gossip of his chief councilors. Hidetsugu had committed suicide on the fifteenth day of the seventh month of the fourth year of Bunroku (1595). On the same day, more than thirty of his ladies had committed suicide at Sanjōgawara. Shortly thereafter, Kimura no Hitachi, Hidetsugu's most trusted retainer, and his wife had also committed suicide. Kimura had an infant daughter in her first year, and Hattori Shōji, who had been Kimura's retainer, had cared for her until her eleventh year when he had died. She had been adopted by Lord Konoe. One day when the ladies in the womens' quarters were celebrating the changing of the month, she had been called upon to perform on the *koto*, and the emperor had been so impressed with her beauty and skill that he had personally given her the name Yuki no Mae. This was the lady whom Uraminosuke had seen at Kiyomizu.

Upon hearing all this, Uraminosuke despairs, believing that his love for the lady is hopeless. Hattori Shōji's widow, however, suggests that their messages from Kannon were a good omen and offers to arrange for a woman called Ayame, Yuki no Mae's closest intimate, to act as Uraminosuke's messenger. The arrangements are made, and Uraminosuke pours out his love in a passionate love letter.

Yuki no Mae is deeply moved by the skill and passion of his message and immediately sends a reply. Uraminosuke is delighted to receive her answer, but finds that he cannot unravel the riddle of her message. He appeals to a person called Sōan, who is a frequent companion in his erotic adventures and a famous poet, and Sōan reveals that the lady is prepared to accept his advances. On the evening of the fifteenth day of the eighth month, Uraminosuke steals into the Konoe palace with the help of the widow and Ayame and makes his way to the lady's private chambers.

His wish fulfilled, Uraminosuke is nevertheless in deep despair because the lady has told him that they can never meet again. He falls gravely ill and is soon on the verge of death. His four friends—Omoinosuke, Koinosuke, Midorinosuke, and Ukiyonosuke— learn that he is near death and come to visit him. He implores them to deliver a last message to Yuki no Mae and expires.

Yuki no Mae receives his message and, unable to bear her grief at his death, commits suicide. Hattori Shōji's widow, Ayame, and all of Yuki no Mae's ladies-in-waiting, like the loyal consorts of Hidetsugu, immediately follow their mistress in death. Deeply impressed by this sad story, those left behind resolve to entomb the ill-starred couple together at Kurodani.

# Old *Jōruri* Librettos
## (*Ko-jōruri Shōhon*)

# 古浄瑠璃正本

Old Jōruri Librettos

(Ko-Jōruri Shōhon)

古浄瑠璃正本

Kanei-era edition, dated the fifth month of Kanei 18 (1641). Published by Kyūhei, a Kyoto publisher. Medium-size book. Second volume of an original two-volume set. Three illustrations, approximately 15.7 cm by 11.0 cm.

An example of the first volume of this edition has not yet been discovered, and neither has an example of a Nara-ehon edition. Therefore the contents of the first three chapters of the story are not known. The following is a summary of chapters four through six.

Chapter Four. Kanra Daibu no Tomomasa is the governor of the province of Kazusa. His house is seized by his neighbor Kagenobu of the province of Shimotsuke, and he is thrown into a dungeon. His wife and his two young sons, Tōinobaru and Kamewaka, manage to escape with the help of his trusted retainer Aasemon no Yasutana. They construct a hut near the summit of Usui Pass and live in hiding.

# Kodaibu 小大夫

## Lady Kodaibu

Kanei-era edition, dated the fifth month of Kanei 18 (1641). Published by Kyūbei, a Kyoto publisher. Medium-size book. Second volume of an original two-volume set. Three illustrations, approximately 15.7 cm by 11.0 cm.

*An example of the first volume of this edition has not yet been discovered, and neither has an example of a* Nara-ehon *edition. Therefore the contents of the first three chapters of the story are not known. The following is a summary of chapters four through six.*

**Chapter Four**: Kanra Daibu no Tomomasa is the governor of the province of Kōzuke. His house is seized by his neighbor Kagenobu of the province of Shimotsuke, and he is thrown into a dungeon. His wife and his two young sons, Tomoharu and Kamewaka, manage to escape with the help of his trusted retainer Ansaemon no Yasutsuna. They construct a hut near the summit of Usui Pass and live in hiding.

After providing for the safety of his master's wife and children, Yasutsuna returns to Kōzuke to attempt to rescue Tomomasa. Tomoharu and Kamewaka are captured by mountain bandits and at first it seems that they will be killed. Fortunately, it turns out that the bandits are also from Kōzuke, and, once they have heard the story of Kagenobu's treachery, they become loyal retainers and help Tomomasa's wife and sons survive in the mountains.

**Chapter Five**: Having returned to Kōzuke, Yasutsuna spies on the dungeon in which his master, Tomomasa, is being held in solitary confinement. The dungeon is well-guarded, however, and he sees no hope of staging an escape. He orders his wife, Kodaibu, to discover a way to enter the household of the prison warden, Nagasawa Genzō. Kodaibu is an extraordinarily clever woman and soon manages not only to enter Genzō's women's quarters but also to rise to the position of a lady-in-waiting of high rank.

Chapter Six: Yodalvu becomes intimate with Genzo and contrives to persuade him to entrust her with the key to Tomonasa's cell. On a stormy night, she approaches the men on guard at Tomonasa's cell and offers them cup after cup of sake until they fall into a deep, drunken stupor. She releases Tomonasa and guides him to Yasutsuna, who carries his master on his back all the way to the hut at Usui Pass. Dispatching one of the former mountain bandits as his emissary, Tomonasa circulates a petition throughout Kozuke and, in only one night, raises an army of more than one thousand of his loyal retainers.

At the head of this force, Tomonasa attacks Kagenobu. His forces rout the enemy, and he manages to capture Kagenobu alive. He travels to the capital and takes his case to the emperor, who grants him an imperial mandate to execute Kagenobu and assume control of his domain. Tomonasa's heir, Tomotaru, is granted the third court rank and appointed to the post of Middle Captain. Tomonasa and his son return to Kozuke, where his family continues to reign to this day.

**Chapter Six**: Kodaibu becomes intimate with Genzō and contrives to persuade him to entrust her with the key to Tomomasa's cell. On a stormy night, she approaches the men on guard at Tomomasa's cell and offers them cup after cup of *sake* until they fall into a deep, drunken stupor. She releases Tomomasa and guides him to Yasutsuna, who carries his master on his back all the way to the hut at Usui Pass. Dispatching one of the former mountain bandits as his emissary, Tomomasa circulates a petition throughout Kōzuke and, in only one night, raises an army of more than one thousand of his loyal retainers.

At the head of this force, Tomomasa attacks Kagenobu. His forces rout the enemy, and he manages to capture Kagenobu alive. He travels to the capital and takes his case to the emperor, who grants him an imperial mandate to execute Kagenobu and assume control of his domain. Tomomasa's heir, Tomoharu, is granted the third court rank and appointed to the post of Middle Captain. Tomomasa and his son return to Kōzuke, where his family continues to reign to this day.

# Chūshō 中 将

## The Story of the Middle Captain Ōhashi

Kanei-era edition. Medium-size book (*hanshibon*). First volume of an original two-volume set. Five illustrations, approximately 17.7 cm by 12.0 cm.

*The second volume of this edition has not yet been discovered. The following summary follows the* tanrokubon *edition for chapters one through four. The contents of the second volume may be determined from a Nara-ehon edition, in which the text of the first four chapters is identical to that of the present edition.*

**Volume One, Chapter One**: Ōhashi no Chūshō, though he had been an ally of the Taira, had saved Minamoto no Yoritomo's life during the Heiji War. After Yoritomo's defeat of the Taira and unification of the country under his government in Kamakura, Ōhashi had been granted the domains of Iki Island and Tsushima Island off the coast of Tsukushi (Kyushu) as a reward. He lives there peacefully until Kajiwara no Kagetoki slanders him to Yoritomo, hoping to make these two rich provinces his own. Kagetoki receives a mandate from Yoritomo and sends his son, Genta Kagesue, to Tsukushi to

summon Ohashi to Kamakura. Genta appears in Tsukushi and politely suggests that Ohashi should visit Kamakura. Ohashi, who has seen through Kagetoki's plot, summons his pregnant wife and bids her a tearful farewell. Leaving behind detailed instructions for the protection of his children, he departs for Kamakura.

Chapter Two: Returning with Genta Kagesue to Kamakura, Ohashi is immediately thrown into prison. Still in Tsukushi, his wife bears him a son, whom she names Manjō. Ohashi had instructed her that if she bore a male child she should send him to a temple. Following her husband's orders, his wife sends Manjō to Kōun-ji, Tsukushi's greatest temple. Manjō is teased mercilessly by the temple pages because he has no father, and he runs away from the temple to return to his mother. She tells him the story of his father's betrayal and of his father's instructions, and Manjō returns to Kōun-ji.

Chapter Three: Bearing a scroll containing the text of the Lotus Sutra bequeathed him by his father, Manjō returns to Kōun-ji and devotes himself to scholarship. Soon he has made himself the most-learned monk at the temple.

summon Ōhashi to Kamakura. Genta appears in Tsukushi and politely suggests that Ōhashi should visit Kamakura. Ōhashi, who has seen through Kagetoki's plot, summons his pregnant wife and bids her a tearful farewell. Leaving behind detailed instructions for the protection of his children, he departs for Kamakura.

**Chapter Two**: Returning with Genta Kagesue to Kamakura, Ōhashi is immediately thrown into prison. Still in Tsukushi, his wife bears him a son, whom she names Maniō. Ōhashi had instructed her that if she bore a male child she should send him to a temple. Following her husband's orders, his wife sends Maniō to Kōun-ji, Tsukushi's greatest temple. Maniō is teased mercilessly by the temple pages because he has no father, and he runs away from the temple to return to his mother. She tells him the story of his father's betrayal and of his father's instructions, and Maniō returns to Kōun-ji.

**Chapter Three**: Bearing a scroll containing the text of the Lotus Sutra bequeathed him by his father, Maniō returns to Kōun-ji and devotes himself to scholarship. Soon he has made himself the most learned monk at the temple.

**Chapter Four**: Maniō resolves to find out what has become of his father. Together with another temple page, Matsuwaka, who was the son of one of his father's servants, he steals away from the temple and makes the long journey to Kamakura.

**Volume Two** (based on the *Nara-ehon* edition, *Ōhashi no Chūshō*): Upon their arrival in Kamakura, Maniō and Matsuwaka make a pilgrimage to the Lower Hachiman Shrine, where they offer a reading of the Lotus Sutra. They encounter Yoritomo's wife and are ordered to appear before Yoritomo.

Maniō appears before Yoritomo and defiantly reveals his identity and the purpose of his journey to Kamakura. Deeply impressed by the boy's filial piety, Yoritomo resolves to spare Ōhashi, who at that very moment is about to be executed at Yuigahama. Ōhashi is released, and after a tearful reunion father and son return to Tsukushi. The Ōhashi family lives happily ever after.

# An Illustrated Catalogue of Extant
## *Tanrokubon* Editions

*The following is a catalogue of all tanrokubon editions of which at least one copy is known to be extant. As much information as possible has been given for each edition. Such information was easily obtained in the case of copies of editions in the author's collection or in those of major university libraries. In the case of some editions in private collections it was virtually impossible to obtain adequate bibliographical data. Unless identified as movable wooden type editions, all editions are woodblock editions. The English titles for the stories, given in parentheses, are something more than translations and represent an attempt to give some idea of the content of each work.*

## Classical Tales (*Ko-monogatari*)
古物語

### *Ise Monogatari* (Tales of Ise)
伊勢物語
Kanei-era (1624–44) edition. Large upright book. Fragment of second volume of two extant. Ten illustrations, approximately 19.0 cm by 14.0 cm (see page 38).

## War Tales (*Gunki Monogatari*)
軍記物語

### *Hōgen Monogatari* (The Tale of Hōgen)
保元物語
Three chapters. Kanei 3 (1626) edition. Large upright book. Three volumes. Illustrations approximately 21.0 cm by 15.5 cm. Also extant is an undated Kanei-era edition. One volume (chapter one) extant. Illustrations approximately 20.0 cm by 15.5 cm (see page 42).

### *Heiji Monogatari* (The Tale of Heiji)
平治物語
Three chapters. Kanei 3 (1626) edition. Large upright book. Three volumes. Illustrations approximately 21.0 cm by 15.5 cm. Also extant is an undated Kanei-era edition. Three chapters. Large upright book. Illustrations approximately 21.0 cm by 15.5 cm (see page 46).

### *Gikeiki* (The Chronicle of Yoshitsune)
義経記
Eight chapters. Early Kanei-era woodblock edition. Eight volumes. Illustrations approximately 20.0 cm by 16.0 cm (see page 52). Also extant are a Kanei 8 (1631) movable wooden type edition and a Kanei 12 (1635) woodblock edition. Volume four of the set in the author's collection is from another undatable woodblock edition entitled *Hōgan Monogatari*.

### *Soga Monogatari* (The Tale of the Soga)
曽我物語
Twelve chapters. Kanei-era edition. Large upright book. Twelve volumes. Illustrations approximately 21.0 cm by 14.5 cm (see page 65). Also extant are an undated Kanei-era movable wooden type edition and a woodblock edition dated Shōhō 3 (1646).

## *Kōwakamai* Librettos (*Kōwaka Bukyoku*)
幸若舞曲

### *Fushimi Tokiwa* (Tokiwa's Flight to Fushimi)
伏見常盤
Kanei-era edition. Large upright book. One volume (incomplete). Four illustrations approximately 19.0 cm by 14.0 cm. Color plates on pages 76 through 80 include illustrations from another edition entitled *Fushimi*. A movable wooden type edition from the Kanei era is also extant.

### *Fue no Maki* (The Story of the Flute Book)
笛の巻
Kanei-era edition. Large upright book. One volume. Illustrations approximately 19.7 cm by 13.5 cm (see page 81).

### *Kagekiyo* (Taira no Kagekiyo)
景清

Kanei-era edition. Large upright book. Two volumes. Sixteen illustrations, approximately 18.5 cm by 14.5 cm (see page 86).

## Oisagashi (The Baggage Search at Naoenotsu)
笈さがし

Kanei-era edition. Large upright book. One volume. Six illustrations, approximately 18.5 cm by 13.5 cm (see page 92). Also extant are a woodblock edition dated Manji 1 (1658) and a Kanei-era movable wooden type edition.

## Izumigajō (The Battle at Izumi Castle)
和泉が城

Kanei-era edition. Large upright book. One volume. Nine illustrations, approximately 18.6 cm by 14.0 cm (see page 96).

## Kosode Soga (The Soga Brothers Receive Kosode Robes)
小袖曽我

Kanei-era edition. Large upright book. Two volumes. Seven illustrations, approximately 19.5 cm by 14.0 cm (see page 100).

## Wada Sakamori (Wada Yoshimori's Drunken Banquet)
和田酒盛

Kanei-era movable wooden type edition. Published by Tsuruya Kyūbei. Large upright book. One volume. Nine illustrations, approximately 19.0 cm by 14.0 cm (see page 104).

## Taishokukan (The Adventures of the Taishokukan)
大織冠

Kanei 12 (1635) edition. Large upright book. Two volumes. Eleven illustrations, approximately 19.5 cm by 15.0 cm (see page 108).

## Manjū (The Story of Manjū)
満仲

Kanei-era edition. Large upright book. Two volumes. Ten illustrations, approximately 19.0 cm by 14.5 cm (see page 112). A Kanei-era movable wooden type edition is also extant.

## Yuriwaka Daijin (Great Minister Yuriwaka Defeats the King of the Devils)
百合若大臣

Kanei-era edition. Large upright book. One volume (only the first of two volumes is extant). Seven illustrations, approximately 19.0 cm by 14.5 cm (see page 116). A Kanei-era movable wooden type edition is also extant.

## Hyōgo (The Story of Kiyomori's Human Sacrifice at Tsukishima in Hyōgo). Also called Tsukishima.
兵庫（築島）

Kanei-era edition. Large upright book. One volume (incomplete). Six illustrations, approximately 18.5 cm by 14.0 cm. Also extant is a Kanei-era movable wooden type edition. Large upright book.

## Eboshiori (Yoshitsune's Capping Ceremony)
烏帽子折

Kanei-era edition. Large upright book. Second of two volumes extant. Three illustrations, approximately 19.0 cm by 15.0 cm. Also extant are copies of the second volume of a slightly different woodblock edition dated Kanei 12 (1635) and fragments of a Kanei-era movable wooden type edition.

*Uma-zoroe* (Minamoto no Yoritomo Reviews His Troops at Izu)

馬ぞろへ

Kanei-era movable wooden type edition. Large upright book. One volume. Four illustrations, approximately 18.5 cm by 14.5 cm.

*Atsumori* (Taira no Atsumori)

敦盛

Kanei-era edition. Large upright book. One volume. Illustrations approximately 19.0 cm by 14.0 cm. A Kanei-era movable wooden type edition and a woodblock edition dated Kanei 12 (1635) are also extant.

*Horikawa Yo-uchi* (The Night Attack on the Horikawa Palace)

堀河夜討

Kanei-era edition. Large upright book. The second of two volumes is extant. Illustrations approximately 19.0 cm by 14.6 cm.

*Shizuka* (The Story of Lady Shizuka)

静

Kanei-era edition. Large upright book. Illustrations approximately 18.9 cm by 14.0 cm.

## Takadachi (The Final Battle at Takadachi)
高館

Kanei-era edition. Large upright book. One volume (incomplete). Eight illustrations, approximately 19.0 cm by 15.0 cm.

## Kirikane Soga (The Young Soga Brothers Escape Execution)
切兼曽我

Kanei-era edition. Large upright book. One volume. Four illustrations, approximately 18.8 cm by 14.3 cm.

## Kamata (Kamata no Masakiyo and Yoshitomo Are Betrayed)
かまた

Kanei-era edition. Large upright book. The second of two volumes is extant. Four illustrations, approximately 18.7 cm by 13.8 cm. A Kanei-era movable wooden type edition is also extant.

## Yo-uchi Soga (The Soga Brothers' Night Attack on Kudō no Suketsune)
夜討曽我

Kanei-era movable wooden type edition. Large upright book. One volume (incomplete). Ten illustrations.

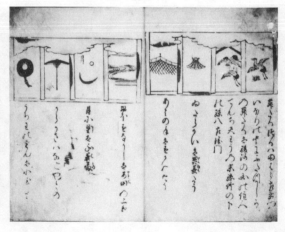

*Yashima* (Benkei Relates the Story of Satō Tsuginobu's Gallant Death at Yashima)

八島

Kanei-era movable wooden type edition. Large upright book. The second of two volumes is extant. Five illustrations. Also extant is a woodblock edition from the Keian or Jōō era with ten illustrations.

*Mongaku* (Mongaku Shōnin and Yoritomo)

文覚

Kanei-era edition. Large upright book. A Kanei-era movable wooden type edition is also extant.

*Tokiwa Mondō* (Lady Tokiwa's Dialogue With Taira no Kiyomori)

常盤問答

Kanei 12 (1635) edition. Large upright book.

*Shida* (The Story of Shida Saburō Senjō [Minamoto no Yoshinobu])

信田

Kanei-era edition. Large upright book.

*Shinkyoku* (New Dance: The Story of Prince Sonryō and the Daughter of the Minister of the Left))

新曲

Kanei-era edition. Large upright book.

*Genbuku Soga* (Soga Jūrō Performs Gorō's Capping Ceremony)

元服曽我

Kanei-era edition. Large upright book.

*Ryūōgashima* (The Island of the Dragon King)

硫王が島

Kanei-era edition. Large upright book.

*Mirai-ki* (The Chronicle of Yoshitsune's Future)

未来記

Kanei-era edition. Large upright book.

*Iruka* (The Story of Soga no Iruka)

入鹿

Kanei-era edition. Large upright book.

*Kiyoshige* (The Tragic Death of Suruga Jirō Kiyoshige)

清重

Kanei-era edition. Large upright book.

*Tsurugi Sandan* (In Praise of Swords)

剣讃嘆

Kanei-era edition. Large upright book.

*Togashi* (Benkei Displays His Wiles at Togashi)

富樫

Kanei-era edition. Large upright book. Also extant is a Kanei-era movable wooden type edition, and a Meireki 4 (1658) edition may also be extant.

## Otogizōshi
御伽草子

*Jūnidan Sōshi* (The Story of Lady Jōruri in Twelve Stages)

十二段草子

Shōhō 3 (1646) edition. Large upright book. Three volumes bound into one (some leaves missing). Nine illustrations, approximately 19.0 cm by 13.5 cm (see page

122). A movable wooden type edition from the Genna era (1615–24) is also extant.

*Chikubujima no Honji* (The Legend of Chikubujima)
竹生島の本地
Genna-era movable wooden type edition. Medium-size upright book. One volume. Four illustrations, approximately 17.5 by 13.5 cm (see page 125).

*Fuji no Hitoana* (The Hole of Man at Mount Fuji)
富士の人穴
Kanei 4 (1627) edition. Large upright book. Two volumes. Sixteen illustrations, approximately 19.5 cm by 14.0 cm (see page 129). Also extant are a movable wooden type edition from the late Genna era or early Kanei era, a woodblock edition dated Kanei 9 (1632), and a woodblock edition dated Keian 3 (1650).

*Kumano no Honji* (The Legend of Kumano)
熊野の本地
Kanei-era edition. Large upright book. Three volumes. Sixty-three illustrations, approximately 20.0 cm by 15.0 cm (see page 134).

*Bunshō Sōshi* (The Story of Bunshō's Good Fortune)
文正草子
Jōō 2 (1653) edition. Large upright book. Two volumes. Twelve illustrations, approximately 20.0 cm by 16.0 cm (see page 141).

*Hioke no Sōshi* (The Story of a Broken Brazier)
火桶の草子
Kanei-era edition. Large upright book. One volume. Eight illustrations, approximately 19.5 by 14.0 cm (see page 145).

*Tengu no Dairi* (Yoshitsune's Visit to the Court of the Great Tengu)
天狗の内裏
Shōhō era (1644–48) edition. Large upright book. Two volumes (some leaves missing). Eleven illustrations, approximately 18.8 cm by 14.8 cm (see page 148).

*Sagoromo* (The Story of Middle Captain Sagoromo)
さごろも
Kanei-era edition. Large upright book. One volume. Fifteen illustrations, approximately 19.0 cm by 14.5 cm (see page 152).

*Hachikazuki* (The Story of Lady Hachikazuki)
鉢かづき
Kanei-era movable wooden type edition. Large upright book. One volume (some leaves missing). Six illustrations, approximately 20.1 cm by 13.9 cm (see page 163).

*Shishō no Uta-awase* (The Poetry Contests of the Four Living Things)
四生の歌合

Kanei-era movable wooden type edition. Large upright book. Two volumes. Fifty-seven illustrations, approximately 27.7 cm by 18.0 cm (see page 167).

*Benkei Monogatari* (The Tale of Benkei)
弁慶物語
Kanei-era movable wooden type edition. Large upright book. One volume. Twelve illustrations.

*Yokobue Takiguchi no Sōshi* (The Story of Yokobue and Takiguchi Nyūdō [Saitō no Tokiyori])
横笛滝口の草子
Late Genna-era or early Kanei-era movable wooden type edition. Large upright book.

*Shijūni no Monoarasoi* (A Poetry Contest in Forty-two Rounds)
四十二の物あらそひ
Early Kanei-era movable wooden type edition; Kanei 4 (1627) woodblock edition; and a Kanei 9 (1632) woodblock edition. Large upright books.

*Sannin Hōshi* (Three Buddhist Priests)
三人法師
Kanei-era movable wooden type edition. Medium-size book. Ten illustrations. Also extant is a woodblock edition dated Kanei 12 (1635).

*Iwaya no Sōshi* (The Story of the Lady Who Lived in a Cave in the Cliffs of Akashi)
岩屋の草子

Keian–Jōō (1648–55) edition. Large upright book. Eight illustrations. A Kanei-era movable wooden type edition is also extant.

*Kachō Fūgetsu* (Kachō and Fūgetsu Stage a Fan Contest)
花鳥風月
Kanei 12 (1635) movable wooden type edition. Large upright book.

*Kibune no Honji* (The Legend of the Kibune Shrine)
貴船の本地
Kanei-era edition. Large upright book.

*Hamaguri no Sōshi* (The Story of the Magical Clam)
蛤の草子
Kanei-era edition. Large upright book.

*Giō* (The Story of Giō and Taira no Kiyomori)
祇王
Kanei-era edition. Large upright book.

*Fukurō* (The Love Affair Between the Patriarch of the Owls and Usohime the Bush Warbler)
ふくろふ
Kanei-era edition. Large upright book.

*Urashima* (The Story of Urashima Tarō and the Magical Turtle)
浦島
Kanei-era edition. Large upright book.

*Karaito Sōshi* (The Story of Lady Karaito)

唐糸草子
Kanei-era edition. Large upright book. A Kanei-era movable wooden type edition is also extant.

*Komachi Sōshi* (The Story of Ono no Komachi)
小町草子
Kanei-era edition. Large upright book. A Kanei-era movable wooden type edition is also extant.

*Tamamushi no Sōshi* (The Jewel Beetle's Book)
玉虫の草子
Kanei-era edition. Large upright book.

*Otaka no Honji* (The Legend of the Otaka Jizō)
おたかの本地
Kanei-era edition. Large upright book. Also called *Monokusa Tarō* (Monokusa Tarō's Good Fortune).

*Gōtō Kijin* (The Robber Devils)
強盗鬼人
Kanei-era edition. Large upright book.

*Wakashu Monogatari* (Edifying Stories for Young Gallants)
若衆物語
Kanei-era edition. Large upright book.

*Tenjin no Honji* (The Legend of the Tenjin Gods)
天神の本地
Keian 1 (1648) edition. Large upright book.

*Shigure* (An Autumn Shower: The Love Story of the Koyoi Captain)
しぐれ
Kanei-era edition. Large upright book.

*Tsukihi no Honji* (The Legend of the Sun and the Moon)
月日の本地
Shōhō–Keian (1644–52) edition. Large upright book. First of two volumes extant. Four illustrations. Also extant is a Kanei-era movable wooden type edition entitled *Tsukimitsu no Sōshi*.

*Kōbō Daishi no Honji* (The Legend of Kōbō Daishi)
弘法大師の本地
Jōō 3 (1654) edition. Large upright book. Three volumes. Twenty-four illustrations.

*Atago Jizō no Monogatari* (The Tale of the Atago Jizō)
愛宕地蔵の物語
Jōō 2 (1653) edition. Large upright book. Second of two volumes extant. Seven illustrations.

*Bishamon-ten no Honji* (The Legend of Bishamon-ten)
毘沙門天の本地
Jōō 3 (1654) edition. Large upright book. Second of three volumes extant. Four illustrations.

*Akashi Monogatari* (The Miraculous Tale of Akashi no Saburō)
明石物語
Jōō–Meireki (1652–1658) edition. Large upright edition. First of two volumes extant. Six illustrations.

*Isozaki* (The Story of Lord Isozaki's Jealous Wife)
磯崎
Meireki-era edition. Large upright book. One volume (incomplete). Five illustrations.

*Tanabata* (The Legend of the Tanabata Festival)
たなばた
Meireki 2 (1656) edition. Large upright book.

*Shaka no Honji* (The Legend of Sakya)
釈迦の本地
Meireki 2 (1656) edition. Large upright book.

*Saru Genji* (Monkey Genji)
猿源氏
Manji 1 (1658) edition. Large upright book.

## Oblong Editions of *Otogizōshi*
横本御伽草子

*Bunshō Sōshi* (The Story of Bunshō's Good Fortune)
文正草子
Undated. Three volumes. In the collection of the Japan Folk Art Museum (gift of Yokoyama Shigeru). Also in the collection of the Japan Folk Art Museum is a copy of the second volume of a three-volume edition of *Bunshō Sōshi*.

*Komachi Sōshi* (The Story of Ono no Komachi)
小町草子
Undated. Second volume of two extant. In the collection of the Waseda University Library.

*Onzōshi Shima-watari* (Yoshitsune's Voyage to Fabulous Islands)
御曹司島渡

Meireki (1655–58) edition. One volume of two extant. Eight illustrations, approximately 13.5 cm by 21.5 cm (see page 156).

*Izumi Shikibu* (The Story of Izumi Shikibu)
和泉式部
Meireki (1655–58) edition. One volume. Five illustrations, approximately 13.0 cm by 22.5 cm (see page 160).

*Nanakusa Sōshi* (The Legend of the Seven Spring Herbs)
ななくさ草子
Undated. In the collection of the Iwasaki Bunko.

*Monogusa Tarō* (The Story of Monogusa Tarō)
ものぐさ太郎
Undated. In the collection of the Kyoto University Library.

*Sazare-ishi* (The Tale of Empress Sazareishi)
さざれいし
Undated. In the collection of the Japan Folk Art Museum.

## *Kanazōshi*
仮名草子

*Usuyuki Monogatari* (The Tale of Lady Usuyuki)
薄雪物語
Kanei 9 (1632) edition. Large upright book. Two volumes. Ten illustrations, approximately 19.5 cm by 15.0 cm (see page 178). A Kanei-era movable wooden type edition is also extant.

*Shichinin Bikuni* (Seven Mendicant Nuns)
七人比丘尼
Kanei 12 (1635) edition. Large upright volume. One volume of two extant. Eleven illustrations, approximately 19.5 cm by 15.0 cm (see page 182). An early Kanei-era movable wooden type edition and a Kanei 9 (1632) woodblock edition are also extant.

*Uraminosuke* (The Story of Uraminosuke)
恨の介
Kanei-era edition. Large upright book. One volume of two extant. Five illustrations, approximately 19.0 cm by 14.1 cm (see page 187).

## *Sekkyō-bushi* Librettos (*Sekkyō-bushi Shōhon*)
説経節正本

*Oguri* (The Story of Oguri Hangan)
をぐり

Early Kanei-era edition. Large upright book. A Kanei-era movable wooden type edition is also extant.

*Karukaya* (The Story of Karukaya Dōshin and Dōnenbō)
かるかや
Kanei 8 (1631) edition. Large upright book. One volume.

*Sanshō Dayū* (The Downfall of Sanshō Dayū)
さんせう太夫
Mid-Kanei-era edition. Large upright book. A Meireki 2 (1656) edition is also extant.

*Shintoku Maru* (Shintoku Maru Is Saved by the Kiyomizu Kannon)
しんとく丸
Shōhō 5 (1649) edition. Large upright book.

## Old *Jōruri* Librettos (*Ko-jōruri Shōhon*)
古浄瑠璃正本

*Kodaibu* (Lady Kodaibu)
小大夫
Kanei 18 (1641) edition. Medium-size upright book. Three illustrations, approximately 15.7 cm by 11.0 cm (see page 192). Sometimes called *Kanra Dayū*.

*Chūshō* (The Story of the Middle Captain Ōhashi). Also called *Ōhashi no Chūsho*.
中将（大橋の中将）
Kanei-era edition. Medium-size upright book. First of two volumes extant. Five illustrations, approximately 17.7 cm by 12.0 cm. (see page 195).

*Jōruri Jūnidan* (The Story of Lady Jōruri in Twelve Stages)
上るり十二段
Late Genna-era (1615–24) movable wooden type edition. Large upright book.

*Takadachi* (The Final Battle at Takadachi)
たかだち
Kanei 2 (1625) edition. Oblong book.

*Hanaya* (The Story of Hanaya the Millionaire)
はなや
Kanei 11 (1634) edition.

*Tōdaiki* (A Chronicle of the Man Who Was Turned into a Candlestick Demon)
燈台鬼
Kanei 12 (1635) edition.

*Tomonaga* (The Tale of Minamoto no Tomonaga)
ともなが
Kanei 14 (1637) edition.

*Akuchi no Hangan* (The Story of the Rich Man of Akuchi)
あくちの判官
Kanei 14 edition.

*Muramatsu* (The Story of Lady Muramatsu and Gojō Mibu Kaneie)
むらまつ
Kanei 14 edition.

*Yashima* (Yoshitsune at Yashima)
八島
Kanei 16 (1639) edition.

*Ada Monogatari* (The Tale of the Sad Love Affair between the Partriarch of the Owls and Usohime the Bush Warbler)
あだ物語
Kanei 17 (1640) edition.

*Ikedori Yo-uchi* (The Night Attack at Ikedori)
いけどり夜討
Kanei 20 (1643) edition.

*Ichinotani Saka-otoshi* (Yoshitsune's Daring Downhill Charge at Ichinotani)
一谷逆落
Kanei 20 edition.

*Taikenmon Heiji Kassen* (The Battle at Taiken Gate in the Heiji War)
待賢門平氏合戦
Kanei 20 edition.

*Amida Honji* (The Legend of the Amida Buddha)
阿弥陀本地
Kanei 21 (1644) edition.

*Ishibashiyama Shichiki-ochi* (Yoritomo's Defeat at Mount Ishibashi)
石橋山七騎落
Kanei-era edition.

*Kosode Soga* (The Soga Brothers Receive *Kosode* Robes)
小袖そが
Late Kanei-era edition. A Shōhō 4 (1647) edition is also extant.

*Kiyoshige* (The Tragic Death of Suruga Jirō Kiyoshige)
きよしげ
Shōhō 2 (1645) edition.

*Akashi* (The Story of Akashi no Saburō)
あかし
Shōhō 2 edition.

*Ko-Atsumori* (The Story of Atsumori's Son)
こあつもり

Shōhō 2 edition.

*Suwa no Honji Kaneie* (The Legend of the Suwa Shrine and the Story of Kaneie)
すわのほんぢ兼家
Shōhō 3 (1646) edition.

*Yorimasa* (The Tragic Story of Minamoto no Yorimasa)
よりまさ
Shōhō 3 edition.

*Harada* (The Story of the Harada Family)
はらだ
Shōhō 4 (1647) edition.

*Amida no Honji* (The Legend of the Amida Buddha)
あみだのほんぢ
Shōhō 4 edition (see *Amida Honji* above).

*Yumitsugi* (The Story of the Shattered Bow)
ゆみつぎ
Shōhō 5 (1648) edition.

*Ozasa* (The Story of Lady Ozasa)
小篠
Undated.

*Kiyomizu no Go-honji* (The Legend of Kiyomizu-dera)
清水の御本地
Keian 4 (1651) edition.

*Munewari* (Amida Nyorai Performs a Miracle)
むねわり
Keian 4 edition.

*Fukiage Hidehira Iri* (Fujiwara no Hidehira Lands at Fukiage)
ふきあげひでひら入
Keian 4 edition.

*Tamura* (The Fabulous Exploits of Sakanoue no Tamura Maru)
たむら
Keian 5 (1652) edition.

*Nichiren-ki* (A Chronicle of Nichiren)
にちれんき
Jōō 3 (1654) edition.

## Picture Scrolls (*Emakimono*)
絵巻物

*Kanei Gyōkōki* (An Imperial Procession of the Kanei Era)
寛永行幸記
A set of three picture scrolls printed in the style of

*tanrokubon*. The scrolls depict the procession of Emperor
Go-Mizunoo to the shogun's Nijō palace during the
Kanei era.

  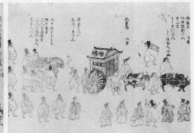

*Gion Sairei Gyōretsu Emaki* (Picture Scroll of the Gion
Festival)
祇園祭礼行列絵巻
Sixteen fragments discovered concealed inside the thick
cover binding of an eight-volume edition of *Gikeiki*
published in 1635.

# Notes

1. The three *tanrokubon* texts reproduced in Tanehiko's *Yōshabako* were the old *jōruri* libretto *Yashima* and two librettos for *sekkyō-bushi*, *Sanshō Dayū* and *Karukaya*.

2. The assignment of dates for the periods in Japanese literature and art history is based on *Nihon Bungaku Zenshi*, 6 vols. (Gakutōsha, 1978), vol. 3, p. 18, which is now considered to be the most authoritative history of Japanese literature. While these dates are based on the founding of the Tokugawa shogunate in 1603 and its fall in 1868, historical rather than literary criteria, it is now thought that they are convenient for literary and art history as well.

3. There was also a genre of fan painting popular during the Heian period in which paintings depicting scenes from Buddhist sutras were done on paper fans (*senmen ko-shakyō*). In some cases, the illustrations were produced by woodblock printing and colors were applied by hand. However, the printing techniques employed in producing these fans were quite primitive, and it is difficult to include them in a discussion of printed illustrations colored by hand.

4. Mizutani Futō, *Kanazōshi* (Taiyōsha, 1919 [reprinted by Chūō Kōron-sha, 1975]).

5. In my discussion of *Nara-e* and *Nara-ehon*, I am indebted to Matsumoto Ryūshin. See, for example, "*Otogizōshi to Nara-ehon*" in *Gotō Bijutsukan Bijutsu Kōza*, no. 23, 1963; *Otogizōshi-shū* (Shinchōsha, 1980); and Yokoyama Shigeru and Matsumoto Ryūshin, *Muromachi Jidai Monogatari Taisei* (Kadokawa Shoten, 1973–80). *Muromachi Jidai Monogatari Taisei* represents a plateau in textual studies of the genres of medieval literature, offering as it does a twelve-volume compendium of some three hundred examples.

   For excellent studies of *Nara-ehon* in English, see: James T. Araki, "*Otogizōshi* and *Nara-ehon*: A Field of Study in Flux," *Monumenta Nipponica*, vol. 36, no. 1, Spring 1981; and Barbara Ruch, "Medieval Jongleurs and the Making of a National Literature," in John W. Hall and Toyoda Takeshi, eds., *Japan in the Muromachi Age* (Berkeley, Calif.: University of California Press, 1977).

6. Kawase Kazuma, *Sagabon-zu Kō* (Isseidō Shoten, 1932).

7. Examples of printed manuscripts in which colors were applied by techniques of printing are extremely rare among books or scrolls from the early Edo period. However, there are a few examples of woodblock editions in which two colors were applied by employing crude printing techniques: *Jingōki* (1631), *Senmeireki* (1644), and *Wakan Gōun-zu* (1645). These were all produced by Yoshida Mitsuyoshi whose family was closely related to the Suminokura family, suggesting that

these early experiments with color printing were connected with the ambitious publishing activities of this wealthy merchant family.

I suspect that the same may be true of the edition entitled *Ouma-in*, which contains polychrome illustrations produced by print techniques and touched up by hand. There is also the theory that this print was produced by exploiting a technique called *kappa-zuri* in which colors were applied by utilizing a technique similar to silk-screen printing. An original painting was done on stiff paper, which was then perforated to allow colors to seep through onto the paper that was to be printed. The "master painting" was then spread over the paper, and colors applied to the "master" in desired places.

8. Tokushi Yūshō, "*Irozuri-bon Zakkō*," *Kinsei Insatsu Bunka-shi* (Ōsaka Shuppan-sha, 1938).

9. Yokoyama Shigeru, "*Katsujibon, E-iribon, Shikisai no Hon*," in *Kokugo to Kokubungaku*, April 1954. See also, Yokoyama Shigeru, "*Otogizōshi*," in Ichiko Teiji and Noma Kōshin, eds., *Otogizōshi, Kanazōshi* (Kadokawa Shoten, 1963).

10. See Kawase, *Sagabon-zu Kō* (note 6). Originally, these texts were in the collections of Mr. Sugiura Kyūen and the Iwasaki Bunko.

11. This essay first appeared in *Mingei*, May 1971.

12. Inoue Kazuo, *Keichō Irai Shoko Shūran* (Shūbundō Shoten, 1916). This book was the result of Inoue's many years of "poking my head into every old book I could find, searching for colophons bearing publishers' seals." Its title might be translated as, "A Survey of Booksellers from the Keichō Era to the Present." Inoue has listed more than one thousand shops specializing in old books. An expanded edition has been published recently by Takao Shoten.

13. James Araki, "*Otogi-zōshi* and *Nara-ehon*: A Field in Flux" (note 5), pp. 16–18. In Japanese, see Miya Tsugio, "*Muromachi Emaki to Nara-ehon*" in *Kaigai Shozō Nara-ehon* (Kōdansha, 1979), pp. 40–43.

14. See Yoshizawa Yoshinori, *Muromachi Bungaku-shi* (Tōkyōdō, 1943).

15. For an account of the performing arts during this period and their relationship to the various literary genres of *Nara-ehon* and *tanrokubon*, see Ichiko Teiji and Kubota Jun, eds., *Nihon Bungaku Zenshi*, vol. 3 (Gakutōsha, 1978), pp. 436–87. Barbara Ruch (note 5) offers a short discussion in English.

16. For a summary of the scholarly debate concerning an appropriate name for this genre, see Ōshima Takehiko, *Otogizōshi-shū, Nihon Bungaku Zenshū*, vol. 36, (Shōgakukan, 1974), pp. 5–34. This volume also contains annotated texts of the twenty-three stories in *Otogi Bunko*.

For a list of extant works, see Matsumoto Ryūshin, ed., *Otogizōshi-shū* (Shinchōsha, 1980), pp. 393–410. This list contains 347 titles, and does not include works in the genres of *kōwakamai* librettos and *sekkyō-bushi* librettos.

Kubota Jun has compiled a complete list of more than 250 titles, which appears in Ichiko Teiji and Noma Kōshin, eds., *Otogizōshi, Kanazōshi* (Kadokawa Shoten, 1963), pp. 330–35.

Barbara Ruch has published part of her detailed study of *Otogi Bunko* in "Origins of the Companion Library: An Anthology of Medieval Japanese Stories," *Journal of Asian Studies*, vol. 30, no. 3, 1971, pp. 593–610.

17. For a more complete discussion, see Ichiko Teiji and Tsutsumi Seiji, eds., *Nihon Bungaku Zenshi*, vol. 4 (Gakutōsha, 1980), pp. 34–51.

18. See note 15.

19. See note 15.

20. The terms *tan-e* and *beni-e*, for example, may be found in Kyokutei (Takizawa) Bakin's *Enseki Zasshi*, published in 1810, and Santō Kyōden's *Kottō-shū*, published in 1813.

21. Miyazaki Harumi, "*Tanrokubon ni tsuite*," in Conference Commemorating the Scholastic Achievements of the late Professor Fujimura Saku, ed., *Kinsei no Bungaku* (Shibundō, 1936). Miyazaki states, "In general, I wonder if we cannot conclude that the term *tanrokubon* was coined not during the Meiji era, but during the Taishō era."

22. Nakada Katsunosuke, *Ehon no Kenkyū* (Bijutsu Shuppan-sha, 1950).

23. Quoted in Ono Tadashige, *Hanga: Nihon no Kurashi no E* (Daviddo-sha, 1958). The author has also received a personal correspondence concerning this entry in Mizutani's encyclopedia from Mr. Inamura Tetsugen.

24. Gift of the late Professor Kōda Shigetomo.

25. Mizutani Futō, *Kanazōshi* (see note 4).

# Glossary

*Ayatsuri ningyō*:

操り人形

A general term for manipulatable puppets. Puppets vary in style and complexity depending on the puppet theater in which they are employed and on historical periods, but the most familiar are those of the Bunraku *jōruri* puppet theater. The most complex bunraku puppets require three highly trained puppet masters to manipulate them on stage.

*Bokashi*:

ぼかし

A technique of applying color to achieve subtle gradations between colors. This technique is employed only rarely in *tanrokubon* illustrations.

*Bukkyō hanga*:

仏教版画

"Buddhist prints." Generally, any woodblock print with Buddhist themes or motifs. Art and literary historians use the term to refer to woodblock prints produced by the Buddhist establishment before the Edo period (1603–1868), when publishing activity was dominated almost exclusively by religious institutions. *Yūzū Nenbutsu Engi* (Ōei era, 1394–1428) is the most famous example.

*Chō*:

丁

One "leaf" of a book. This term corresponds roughly to the English word "signature." It refers to an uncut sheet of paper in any of the traditional styles of binding. In the *fukuro toji* style of binding, which has been employed in the present volume, a *chō* is one sheet of paper folded in half with the printing on the outside, comprising two pages of text and illustration. The open edges of the "leaves" are sewn together so that the book opens from the folds. (See *Fukuro toji* and *Kochōsō* below.)

*Chūbon*:

中本

"Medium-size upright books." Also called *hanshibon*. One of the formats of *tanrokubon*. The usual dimensions of these books are 24 cm in height by 17 cm in width.

*Daikashira-ryū*:

大頭流

One of the two traditions of *kōwakamai* performance. In the *daikashira-ryū* performance style there are three performers. Founded by Jirōzaemon Naoyoshi of Echizen, *daikashira-ryū* performances can still be seen in the village of Ōe in Fukuoka Prefecture. (See *Kō-waka-ryū* below.)

Eiribon

絵入本

A book with illustrations. One of the old terms for "ehon."

Ehon

絵本

A general term for a picture book, whether modern or traditional. The term "ehon" implies much more emphasis on illustration than the term "ezōshi."

Eiri kappon

絵入活本

"Illustrated printed edition." This is a general term referring to printed books with illustrations published during the Edo period.

Emakimono

絵巻物

A general term referring to any illustrated scroll.

Ezōshi

絵草紙

A general term for pre-modern picture books. Like the term "ehon," it implies a much heavier emphasis on illustrations than such terms as "ehon."

Fukuro toji

袋綴

The style of book binding employed in annotation, as well as the vast majority of other pre-modern Japanese books. Each sheet of paper is folded in half, with the hand-written or printed text and illustrations on the outside of each "leaf." Leaves are then sewn together at the open edges opposite the fold. Fukuro toji has been employed in the binding of the present volume.

Fukinuki yatai

吹抜屋台

A style of depicting interior scenes in which portions of walls or ceilings are omitted to afford views of interiors. The technique of fukinuki yatai is characteristic of Yamato-e painting styles.

Fushimi-ban

伏見版

The Fushimi-ban were editions of the Chinese classics, Japanese literature and Chinese (kan-seki), and official documents (kansho) printed at Tokugawa Ieyasu's (1542–1616) the self-behind. (See anotation below.)

Gunki monogatari

軍記物語

"War tales." A genre of medieval Japanese literature that encompasses the highly lyrical war tales written during the Kamakura period, such as Heike Monogatari, as well as the popular tales of heroism and adventure written during the Muromachi period, such as

*Edoribon*:

絵どり本

A book with illustrations. One of the old terms for *tanrokubon*.

*Ehon*:

絵本

A general term for a picture book, whether modern or traditional. The term *ehon* implies much more emphasis on illustration than the term *eiribon*.

*E-iri kanpon*:

絵入刊本

"Illustrated printed editions." This is a general term referring to printed books with illustrations published during the Edo period.

*Emakimono*:

絵巻物

A general term referring to any illustrated scroll.

*E-zōshi*:

絵草紙

A general term for pre-modern picture books. Like the term *ehon*, it implies a much heavier emphasis on illustrations than such terms as *e-iribon*.

*Fukuro toji*:

袋綴

The style of book binding employed in *tanrokubon*, as well as the vast majority of other pre-modern Japanese books. Each sheet of paper is folded in half with the hand-written or printed text and illustrations on the outside of each "leaf." Leaves are then sewn together at the open edges opposite the fold. *Fukuro toji* has been employed in the binding of the present volume.

*Fukinuki yatai*:

吹抜屋台

A style of depicting interior scenes in which portions of walls or ceilings are omitted to afford views of interiors. The technique of *fukinuki yatai* is characteristic of *Yamato-e* painting styles.

*Fushimi-ban*:

伏見版

The *Fushimi-ban* were editions of the Chinese classics, Japanese literature in Chinese (*kan-bun*), and official documents (*komonjo*) printed at Tokugawa Ieyasu's (1542–1616) castle at Fushimi. (See *Suruga-ban* below.)

*Gunki monogatari*:

軍記物語

"War tales." A genre of medieval Japanese literature that encompasses the highly lyrical war tales written during the Kamakura period, such as *Heike Monogatari*, as well as the popular tales of heroism and adventure written during the Muromachi period, such as

*Gikeiki.* The heroes and themes of the war tales provided subjects for many of the other genres of medieval literature, as well as for popular art, and they continued to do so through the Edo period and into the modern age.

## *Hanshibon:*
半 紙 本
An alternative, though mistaken, term used to refer to medium-size upright books (*chū-bon*). The name derives from the fact that *hanshi*, a type of paper employed in some editions is very similar in size to that employed in true *chūbon*. (See *chūbon* above.)

## *Honji, honjimono:*
本 地、本 地 物
The term *honji* refers to a type of prose narrative that can be traced back to Japan's earliest literature and proto-history. *Honji* relate the legends or myths surrounding the origins of Buddhist temples, Shintō shrines, deities, Buddhas, place names, saints, the sun and the moon, popular religious beliefs, and so on. The legends and myths overlap with quasi-historical fact in a complicated web of contradictions. Even within the limited repertoire of *sekkyō-bushi* librettos, for example, one finds dozens of explanations for the origins of the Kiyomizu Kannon. *Honji* motifs also pervade the other genres of medieval literature. The Soga brothers, for example, are found stopping at famous places along the way to their fateful encounter on the plain below Mount Fuji to recall the legends of these places. The popularity of *honji* is explained in part by the fact that they were a major part of the repertoire of wandering monks and nuns, who performed *sekkyō-bushi* and other forms of recitational art at temple gates throughout the medieval period.

## *Irodori-eiri:*
色 ど り 絵 入
A printed edition that includes hand-colored illustrations.

## *Iro-dori saishiki:*
色 ど り 彩 色
A printed edition with illustrations colored by hand.

## *Kabuse-bori:*
覆 刻
*Kabuse-bori* is a technique of reproducing woodblocks by spreading a print made from the original block over a new one and engraving an exact copy. This technique was also employed in preparing woodblocks based on movable wooden type prints. One consequence of this practice is that woodblock prints produced in this way can be easily mistaken for movable wooden type prints.

## *Kanazōshi:*
仮 名 草 子
*Kanazōshi* is the term that has gained currency among specialists to refer to texts of fictional narrative considered to be transitional from true *otogizōshi* of the Muromachi period (1392–1573) to the *ukiyozōshi* of the Edo period (1603–1868), a genre that is considered to have begun with the publication of Ihara Saikaku's *Kōshoku Ichidai Otoko* (The Man Who Loved Love) in 1685.

*Kanbun*:

漢 文

*Kanbun* is the Japanese word for a text written in classical Chinese, including the Chinese classics and texts written by Japanese. *Kanbun* is read as classical Japanese by using a complicated system of diacritical marks.

*Kawaraban*:

瓦 版

*Kawaraban* editions are books printed by a technique in which the text and illustrations are carved on clay blocks that are then baked or dried. This relatively inexpensive printing technique was employed extensively throughout the Edo period by townsman newspaper publishers.

*Kochōsō*:

胡 蝶 装

*Kochōsō*, or "butterfly binding," is the style of binding characteristic of *Nara-ehon*. It is thought to have been modeled on books that were being imported from Ming China during the period. Each sheet of paper is folded in half, with hand-written or printed text and illustrations on the inside of each "leaf." Leaves are then pasted together at the folded edges. The term "butterfly binding" derives from the fact that the facing pages of text stand out from the rest of the book when opened. This binding technique is thus the direct opposite of the technique of *fukuro toji* employed in *tanrokubon*.

*Kohon*:

小 本

"Small-size books." One of the formats of *tanrokubon*. The average dimensions of these editions are 19.5 cm in height and 14 cm in width.

*Ko-katsuji*:

古 活 字

"Old movable wooden type printing." Movable type from two independent sources appeared in Japan almost simultaneously. The Jesuit Mission Press, which employed a copperplate type press, published the first *Kirishitan-ban* (Christian books) in 1591 and Toyotomi Hideyoshi brought back the first movable wooden type press from his Korean campaign in 1592, along with a Korean version of the copperplate press. The techniques of movable wooden type printing developed rapidly and, with the publication of the *Sagabon* editions, it became so popular that woodblock printing virtually disappeared. This development came to an abrupt end around 1650, however, as the explosion of demand for books made movable wooden type printing increasingly unprofitable.

*Komonjo*:

古 文 書

*Komonjo* is a modern term referring to old hand-written historical documents.

*Ko-monogatari*:

古 物 語

This term refers to *monogatari*, or tales, that had already become classics by the time *Nara-ehon*, the *Sagabon* editions, and *tanrokubon* were being produced. While only *Ise Monogatari* is represented by a *tanrokubon* edition, the term also encompasses *The Tale of Genji* (*Genji Monogatari*) and other great works of the Heian period (794–1185).

## *Kōwakamai* librettos (*Kōwaka bukyoku* or *mai no hon*):
幸 若 舞 曲
A dance theater that evolved from *kusemai*, *kōwakamai* developed into a stage art during the period of almost constant warfare preceding the Edo Period (1603–1868). *Kōwakamai* librettos drew their dramatic material from medieval war tales and related legends and were also read as fictional narratives.

## *Kōwaka-ryū*:
幸 若 流
The *kōwaka-ryū* is one of the two traditions of *kōwakamai*. It traces its history back to Kōwaka Maru, who is traditionally held to be the originator of *kōwakamai*. The *kōwaka-ryū* style of performance can no longer be seen, but the distinction between this school and that of the *daikashira-ryū* is important because there are also two separate textual histories of *kōwakamai* librettos. (See *Daikashira-ryū* above.)

## *Kusemai*:
曲 舞
*Kusemai* was a dance theater performed at temple gates during the Muromachi period (1392–1573). It exerted an enormous influence on the evolution of the Nō theater during the Azuchi–Momoyama period (1573–1603) and itself developed into the popular stage art *kōwakamai*. Because it was performed by two dancers, it was also called *maimai* (dance dance) and *futari mai* (two people's dance).

## *Machi-eshi*:
町 絵 師
The term *machi-eshi* can be extremely misleading. Literally, it means "townsman painter," but some of the *machi-eshi* were *samurai* of high rank. The term may best be understood as one referring to painters who were not formally associated with one of the officially recognized schools and who worked in popular genres of painting. Unlike the painters of the official schools, most of these artists remain buried in obscurity. The artists of the *Sagabon*, *Nara-ehon*, and *tanrokubon* editions are completely unknown, and even the lives of such masters as Utamaro and Sharaku are shrouded in enigma. Nevertheless, the view of modern art historians is that the *machi-eshi* dominated Japanese painting throughout the Edo period (1603–1868).

## *Maniai-gami*:
間 以 合 紙
*Maniai-gami* is similar to *torinoko-gami* but is of a slightly lesser quality. *Torinoko-gami* is more common in early *Nara-ehon*, while *maniai-gami* is characteristic of later "folk style" *Nara-ehon*.

## *Mino-ban*:
美 濃 版
"Mino books." An alternative term for large-size upright books (*ōbon*). The name derives from the fact that Mino paper was often employed in these books. (See *Ōbon* below.)

### Nanto-e:
南都絵

"Southern capital paintings." A term suggested by some specialists as an alternative for *Nara-e*. Since Nara was the "southern capital," the distinction is meaningless.

### Nara-e:
奈良絵

"Nara pictures." This term refers to a genre of paintings similar to the illustrations in *Nara-ehon*. One theory holds that these paintings were produced by artists associated with the Kasuga Shrine in Nara, while another suggests that the priests of the Buddhist establishment in Nara themselves published these popular paintings as a sideline to their work on Buddhist prints.

### Nara-ehon
奈良絵本

*Nara-ehon* is the term that has gained currency among literary and art historians to refer to a type of hand-copied books or scrolls with original color illustrations, published from about 1450 to the early eighteenth century. The literary genres of *Nara-ehon* are almost identical to those of *tanrokubon*. However, there are radical differences in painting styles and techniques of coloring. The meticulous realism of coloring in *Nara-ehon* illustrations contrasts sharply with the rather artless abstraction of *tanrokubon* illustrations.

### Nishiki-e:
錦絵

"Brocade prints." *Nishiki-e* is the genre of woodblock prints that comes to mind most quickly when one thinks of *ukiyo-e* prints, which in fact is a much broader genre classification including monochrome as well as color prints. *Nishiki-e* represent the technical perfection of the woodblock print, employing large numbers of woodblock prints to produce polychrome prints with nothing added by hand. Surprisingly, given the rather slow evolution of woodblock printing, the transition from woodblock prints with color added by hand to *nishiki-e* occurred in the space of only one year, with the beautiful prints of Suzuki Harunobu (1725–70). The term *nishiki-e* was suggested by the gorgeous Shujiang brocades (*Shokkō nishiki*) popular during the period.

### Ōbon:
大本

"Large-size upright book." Also referred to as *Mino-ban*. One of the formats of *tanrokubon*. The usual dimensions of these books are 28 cm by 28 cm. (See *Mino-ban* above.)

### Old jōruri librettos (ko-jōruri shōhon):
古浄瑠璃正本

The term old *jōruri* refers to the *Jōruri*, or Bunraku, puppet theater as it existed in the period of roughly seventy-five years from the late Keichō era (1596–1615) to 1684, when the *jōruri* theater was transformed by the revolutionary new librettos of Chikamatsu Monzaemon. *Jōruri* traces its tradition to the middle of the fifteenth century, when wandering nuns (*bikuni*) developed a unique chanting style for oral recitations of *Jōruri Jūnidan Sōshi* (The Story of Lady Jōruri in Twelve Stages). Old *jōruri* librettos are printed or handwritten texts of the plays denuded of musical and recitational neumes.

*Otogi bunko*:

御 伽 文 庫

Twenty-three volume editions of *otogizōshi* published by Shibukawa Seiemon in Osaka during the Kyōhō era (1716–36). While these editions have monochrome illustrations, the original woodblocks may have been used to produce *tanrokubon* in Kyoto during the Kanei era.

*Otogizōshi*:

御 伽 草 子

The term *otogizōshi* is the subject of a great deal of scholarly debate. Some specialists reject it completely, while others would expand its definition to include almost all of the genres of popular medieval fiction. In this study of *tanrokubon*, the term refers to a genre of short narrative fiction written during the Muromachi and Momoyama periods (1392–1603) and the early decades of the Edo period. This definition distinguishes *otogizōshi* from the librettos for the dance theaters *kōwakamai* and *sekkyō-bushi*.

*Roku*:

緑

A green pigment obtained by mixing powdered malachite and water.

*Sagabon*:

嵯 峨 本

The *Sagabon* editions were published in the latter half of the Keichō era (1596–1615) by the wealthy Kyoto merchants Honami Kōetsu and Suminokura Soan, and were called *Sagabon* because Soan lived in the Saga district of Kyoto. The *Sagabon* editions were the first true printed books with illustrations in the Japanese tradition. Most of the *Sagabon* were movable wooden type editions with monochrome woodblock illustrations, although there is evidence of at least one woodblock edition, an edition of the *Sagabon Ise Monogatari*. Besides *Ise Monogatari*, the *Sagabon* collections of classical literature included twelve other titles, including a treatise on *The Tale of Genji* and several collections of Nō plays and *waka* poetry.

*Saiga-iri*:

彩 画 入

A book with color illustrations.

*Seihanbon*:

整 版 本

Woodblock-printed books. The techniques of woodblock printing dominated publishing activity almost exclusively after 1650.

*Suruga-ban*:

駿 河 版

Editions printed at Tokugawa Ieyasu's castle at Suruga. (See *Fushimi-ban* above.)

*Suyari-gasumi*:

す や り 霞

A decorative technique employed in *Yamato-e* painting styles in which stylized cloud pat-

terns intrude into the scenes depicted in a variety of interesting ways. The same technique is also used in *tanrokubon* to separate two scenes that appear in the same illustration.

*Sekkyō-bushi* librettos (*sekkyō-bushi shōhon*):
説経節正本
*Sekkyō-bushi* developed at the end of the Kamakura period (1185–1392) or the beginning of the Muromachi period (1392–1573) as a form of oral recitation performed by priests and nuns involved in evangelical work among the lower classes. It emerged as a stage art during the Keichō era (1596–1615), when performers began to employ a type of puppet that could be manipulated and more sophisticated chanting styles, and enjoyed its greatest vogue during the Kanei era (1624–44).

*Tan*:
丹
An orange-red pigment obtained by mixing powdered red lead with water.

*Tan-e*:
丹絵
*Tan-e*, or "orange-red prints," which were published in the period from the end of the Genroku era (1688–1704) to the beginning of the Kyōhō era (1716–36), represent the first attempt to add color to single-sheet *ukiyo-e* prints. It is here that the influence of *tanrokubon* illustrations on *ukiyo-e* may be most clearly seen. Two or three colors—orange-red (*tan*), mineral green (*roku*), and yellow (*ki*)—were applied with an extremely rough hand to a monochrome print, employing precisely the same techniques as in *tanrokubon*.

*Tanroku-eiribon*:
丹緑絵入本
One of the terms used in the late Meiji era (1868–1912) to refer to *tanrokubon*. Literally, it means "books with orange-red and mineral green illustrations."

*Tanroku-saiiri*:
丹緑彩入
A term less common than *tanroku-eiribon*, used in the Meiji period to refer to *tanrokubon*. It might be translated "books with orange-red and mineral green color."

*Tanshokudori-bon*:
丹色どり本
An edition with illustrations hand-colored with orange-red.

*Torinoko-gami*:
鳥の子紙
A good quality paper of egg-shell hue with a hard lustrous surface, *torinoko-gami* is characteristic of early *Nara-ehon* editions.

*Urushi-e*:
漆絵
*Urushi-e*, or "lacquer prints," mark an advance in the technique of printing monochrome

illustrations itself. In the period between 1720 and 1730, a rose-red pigment called *beni* replaced orange-red and mineral green as the favorite of artists and printers for adding color to woodblock prints, and *beni-e*, or "rose prints," replaced *tan-e* as the most popular genre of *ukiyo-e*. *Urushi-e* represent the next stage of development, in which printers began to use black ink with an extremely high glue content, producing a lustrous effect suggestive of Japanese lacquerware.

*Yamato-e*:

大和絵

*Yamato-e* is a general term that distinguishes indigenous Japanese painting styles from those heavily influenced by Chinese painting. Among "official" schools of painting, the painting styles of the Tosa school are most closely associated with *Yamato-e*. The anonymous *machi-eshi* who produced *tanrokubon*, as well as their successors in the various schools of *ukiyo-e*, also found their inspiration in the *Yamato-e* style of painting.

*Yokohama-e*:

横浜絵

*Yokohama-e* constitute a subgenre of *nishiki-e*. Published at the end of the Edo period (1603–1868) and the beginning of the Meiji era (1868–1912), these prints often depict foreigners in Japan. It is perhaps for this reason that they came to be called *Yokohama-e*, since the port of Yokohama was widely known for its large foreign population. It is highly unlikely that all or even most of the *Yokohama-e* were actually published in Yokohama.

*Yokohon*:

横本

"Oblong books." One of the formats of *tanrokubon*, *Nara-ehon*, and later monochrome books. Oblong *tanrokubon* editions are usually 15.6 cm in height and 23 cm in width. A number of old *jōruri* librettos and editions in a subcategory of *otogizōshi* are in this format.

# Selected Bibliography

Araki, James T. "*Otogi-zōshi* and *Nara-ehon*: A Field in Flux." *Monumenta Nipponica*, vol. 36, no. 1 (Spring 1981): 1–20.

———. "*Bunshō Sōshi*: The Tale of Bunshō, the Saltmaker." *Monumenta Nipponica*, vol. 38, no. 3 (Autumn 1983): 221–50.

Ichiko, Teiji. *Chūsei Shōsetsu no Kenkyū*. Tokyo: Tōkyō Daigaku Shuppankan, 1955.

Ichiko Teiji, ed. *Otogizōshi*. *Nihon Koten Bungaku Taikei*, vol. 38. Tokyo: Iwanami Shoten, 1958.

Ichiko, Teiji, ed. *Nihon Bungaku Zenshi*, vol. 3, *Chūsei* and vol. 4, *Kinsei*. Tokyo: Gakutōsha, 1978.

Ichiko, Teiji, and Noma, Kōshin, eds. *Otogizōshi, Kanazōshi*. Tokyo: Kadokawa Shoten, 1963.

Ichiko, Teiji, and Ōshima, Tatehiko, eds. *Soga Monogatari*. *Nihon Koten Bungaku Taikei*, vol. 88. Tokyo: Iwanami Shoten, 1966.

Inoue, Kazuo. *Keichō Irai Shoko Shūran*. Tokyo: Shūbundō Shoten, 1916.

Jinbo, Kazuya, ed. *Kanazōshi, Ukiyozōshi Shū*. *Nihon Koten Bungaku Zenshū*, vol. 37. Tokyo: Shōgakukan, 1971.

Kajiwara, Masaaki, ed. *Gikeiki*. *Nihon Koten Bungaku Zenshū*, vol. 31. Tokyo: Shōgakukan, 1971.

Kawase, Kazuma. *Sagabon-zu Kō*. Tokyo: Isseidō Shoten, 1932.

Maeda, Kingorō, and Morita, Takeshi, eds. *Kanazōshi Shū*. *Nihon Koten Bungaku Taikei*. vol. 90. Tokyo: Iwanami Shoten, 1965.

Matsumoto, Ryūshin, ed. *Otogizōshi Shū*. Tokyo: Shinchōsha, 1980.

———. "*Otogizōshi to Nara-ehon*." *Gotō Bijutsukan Bijutsu Kōza*, no. 23 (1963).

McCullough, Helen Craig. *Yoshitsune: A Fifteenth Century Japanese Chronicle*. Stanford, Calif.: Stanford University Press, 1966.

———. *Tales of Ise: Lyrical Episodes from Tenth Century Japan*. Stanford, Calif.: Stanford University Press, 1968.

Mitani, Eiji, and Sekine, Yoshiko, ed. *Sagoromo Monogatari*. *Nihon Koten Bungaku Taikei*, vol. 79. Tokyo: Iwanami Shoten, 1965.

Miya, Tsugio. "*Muromachi Emaki to Nara-ehon*." *Kaigai Shozō Nara-ehon*. Tokyo: Kōdansha, 1979.

Miyazaki, Harumi. "*Tanrokubon ni tsuite*." In *Kinsei no Bungaku*, edited by the Conference Commemorating the Scholastic Achievements of the late Professor Fujimura Saku. Tokyo: Shibundō, 1936.

Mizutani, Futō. *Kanazōshi*. Tokyo: Taiyōsha, 1919 (reprinted by Chūō Kōron-sha, 1975).

Nagazumi, Yasuaki, and Shimada, Isao, ed. *Hōgen Monogatari, Heiji Monogatari. Nihon Koten Bungaku Taikei*, vol. 31. Tokyo: Iwanami Shoten, 1961.

Nakada, Katsunosuke. *Ehon no Kenkyū*. Tokyo: Bijutsu Shuppan-sha, 1950.

Ono, Tadashige. *Hanga: Nihon no Kurashi no E*. Tokyo: Daviddo-sha, 1958.

Ōoka, Makoto. "*Otogizōshi.*" *Kaishaku to Kanshō*, vol. 13, no. 7 (June 1968): 91–95.

————. "*Kotoba ni Hana o Sakasu Koto.*" *Bungaku*, vol. 44, no. 9 (September 1976): 132–35.

Ōshima, Takehiko, ed. *Otogizōshi-shū. Nihon Koten Bungaku Zenshū*, vol. 36. Tokyo: Shōgakukan, 1974.

Ruch, Barbara. "Medieval Jongleurs and the Making of a National Literature." In *Japan in the Muromachi Age*, edited by John W. Hall and Toyoda Takeshi, 279–309. Berkeley, Calif.: University of California Press, 1977.

————. "Origins of the Companion Library: An Anthology of Medieval Japanese Stories." *Journal of Asian Studies*, vol. 30, no. 3 (1971): 593–610.

————. "*Sekai no naka no Otogizōshi.*" In *Zusetsu Nihon no Koten*, 181–89. Tokyo: Shūeisha, 1980.

Steven, Chigusa. "*Hachikazuki*: A Muromachi Short Story." *Monumenta Nipponica*, vol. 32, no. 3 (Autumn 1977): 303-31.

Tokushi, Yūshō. "*Irozuri-bon Zakkō.*" In *Kinsei Insatsu Bunka-shi*. Osaka: Shuppan-sha, 1938.

Yokoyama, Shigeru. "*Katsujibon, E-iribon, Shikisai no Hon.*" *Kokugo to Kokubungaku* (April 1954).

Yokoyama, Shigeru, and Matsumoto, Ryūshin, eds. *Muromachi Jidai Monogatari Taisei*. Tokyo: Kadokawa Shoten, 1973–80.

Yoshizawa, Yoshinori. *Muromachi Bungaku-shi*. Tokyo: Tōkyōdō, 1943.

Yūda, Yoshio. *Bunraku Jōruri-shū. Nihon Koten Bungaku Taikei*, vol. 99. Tokyo: Iwanami Shoten, 1965.

# Index

Benkei, 56, 61, 92, 95, 151
*bokashi*, 22
Buddhist prints, 12, 15
*Bunshō Sōshi*, 28, 141–44
*Buppō Shōshūki*, 14
*Bussei Biku Rokumotsu-zu*, 14

Chikamatsu Monzaemon, 30
*Chikubujima no Honji*, 125–28
*chō*, 18
*chūbon. See* Medium-size upright
  books
*Chūshō*, 195–97
classical tales, *tanrokubon* editions of,
  26, 37–40
colophons, 16, 24, 35
colors, application of, by hand,
  11–12, 15, 21
colors, number of, in *tanrokubon*,
  21–22
colors, techniques of application, 22
covers, 13, 19, 22

devotional prints, 22

*edoribon*, 11, 32, 33, 34, 35
*e-iri kanpon*, 11
*emakimono. See* Scrolls

*Fue no Maki*, 81–85
*Fuji no Hitoana*, 129–33
Fujiwara no Hidehira. *See* Hidehira,
  Fujiwara no
*fukinuki yatai*, 20
*fukuro toji*, 18
*Fushimi-ban*, 24
*Fushimi Tokiwa*, 76–80

*Garakuta Bunko*, 32
*Gikeiki*, 18, 19, 26, 27, 30, 34,
  52–64, 92
*Gion Sairei Gyōretsu E-maki*, 30
*Gokyō*, 14
Go-Shirakawa, 42, 45, 46
*Gotō Kijin*, 22
*gunki monogatari. See* War tales

*Hachikazuki*, 163–66
*hanshibon. See* Medium-size upright
  books
*Heiji Monogatari*, 26, 33, 46–51, 52
Hidehira, Fujiwara no, 51, 55, 61,
  96, 99, 156, 159
*Hioke no Sōshi*, 145–47
*Hōgen Monogatari*, 26, 33, 42–45

Honami Kōetsu, 14, 20
*honji*, 29

*Ise Monogatari, Sagabon* edition of,
  12, 14–16, 19, 20
*Ise Monogatari, tanrokubon* edition of,
  20, 26, 38–40
*Izumigajō*, 96–99
*Izumi Shikibu*, 160–62

*jōruri* theater, 30
*Jūgyū-zu*, 14
*Jūnidan Sōshi*, 12, 122–24
*Jūni Ten-zō*, 12

*kabuse-bori*, 31
*Kadensho*, 14
*Kagekiyo*, 34, 86–91
*Kajiwara no Kagetoki*, 60, 99, 151,
  195, 196
*kanazōshi, tanrokubon* editions of, 16,
  20, 29, 177–90
*Kanei Gyōkōki*, 18, 30, 31
Kanō school, 13, 19, 20
*kawaraban* edition, 16
*Kenyūsha*, 32
Kiyomori, Taira no, 45, 51, 52, 55
*Kōbō Daishi Gohonji*, 34
*kochōsō* binding, 13
*Kodaibu*, 192–94
*ko-katsuji. See* Movable wooden type
  printing
*ko-monogatari. See* Classical tales
*Kosode Soga*, 100–103
*kōwakamai* dance theater, 25, 27
*kōwakamai* librettos, *tanrokubon* editions of, 16, 18, 20, 27, 75–120
*Kōya Daishi Gyōjō Zuga*, 12, 31
*Kumano no Honji*, 18, 19, 34,
  134–40
*Kunshin Zuzō*, 14
*kusemai*, 27
Kyoto, *tanrokubon* published in, 25

large upright books, 12, 13, 14, 18
literary genres in *tanrokubon*, 26–30

*machi-eshi. See* Townsman painters
*maniai-gami*, 13, 22, 28
*Manjū*, 34, 112–15
medium-size upright books, 18
Minamoto. *See under personal names*
mineral green (*roku*), 11, 16, 21, 30,
  35
*Mino-ban*, 18

Mizutani Futō, 12, 32, 35
movable wooden type printing, 14,
  17, 24, 30–31

*nanto-e*, 13
*Nara-e*, 13, 20, 21
*Nara-ehon*, 12–14, 15, 25, 26, 35
*nishiki-e*, 17

oblong books, 12, 13, 18, 28–29
*ōgatabon. See* Large upright books
*Oisagashi*, 92–95
*Ōiso no Tora*, 68, 104, 106–7
Okimori Naosaburō, 32–33
old *jōruri* librettos, *tanrokubon* editions for, 11, 16, 18, 25, 30
old movable type editions, 16
*Ongyōkō Shidai*, 33
*Onzōshi Shima-watari*, 156–59
orange-red (*tan*), 11, 16, 21, 30, 35
*Ōsaka Abe no Kassen*, 27
*Otogi Bunko*, 22, 28–29
*otogizōshi*, literary genre of, 23, 26,
  27, 29
*otogizōshi, tanrokubon* editions of, 16,
  18, 20, 27–28, 121–76

print technology, 17, 24, 25, 30–31
publishers of *tanrokubon*, 21–22, 23,
  25
puppet theaters, 25

readers of *tanrokubon*, 25–26
*roku. See* Mineral green
*Ryōgai Mandara*, 12
Ryūtei Tanehiko, 11, 32

*Sagabon* editions, 12, 14–16, 19,
  20, 24
*Sagoromo*, 152–55
Saikaku, Ihara, 29
*saishikibon*, 32
*Sannin Hōshi*, 33
*sanshokubon*, 35
*Saru Genji*, 34
*Sazare-ishi*, 34
scrolls, illustrated, 12, 14, 30
*sekkyō-bushi* librettos, *tanrokubon* edi-
  tions of, 11, 16, 18, 25, 29–30
*Sendensho*, 14
Shibukawa Seiemon, 22, 28
*Shichinin Bikuni*, 29, 182–86
Shikada Shōundō. *See* Shōundō,
  Shikada
*Shingon Hasso-zō*, 12

*Shishō no Uta-awase*, 18, 33, 167–76
Shōundō Shikada, 33–35
*Shūkaishō*, 14
small-size books, 18
*Soga Monogatari*, 18, 19, 26, 27, 31, 34, 65–74
Soga no Gorō Tokimune (Hakoō), 65–68, 100, 103, 107
Soga no Jūrō Sukenari (Ichiman), 67–68, 100, 103, 106–7
Sugimoto Ryōkōdō, 35
Suminokura Soan, 14, 15
Suruga-ban, 24
*suyari-gasumi*, 20, 21

Taira no Kiyomori. *See* Kiyomori, Taira no
*Taishokukan*, 34, 108–11
*Takadachi*, 18
*tan. See* Orange-red
*tan-e*, 17, 19, 33
*tanrokubon*, covers and bindings of, 19, 22
*tanrokubon*, datable, 16
*tanrokubon*, decline of, 16
*tanrokubon*, evolution of term, 34–35
*tanrokubon*, format of 17–18
*tanrokubon* illustrations, arrangement of, 18–19
*tanrokubon* illustrations, colors in, 21–23
*tanrokubon* illustrations, original paintings for, 21
*tanrokubon* illustrations, style of, 20–21
*tanrokubon*, illustrators of, 19–21
*tanrokubon*, influences on, 14, 15, 21
*tanrokubon*, nature of, 11, 20–21
*tanrokubon*, number of illustrations in, 18
*tanrokubon*, origins of, 12, 16
*tanrokubon*, origins of term, 32–33, 35
*tanroku-edoribon*, 34, 35
*tanroku-eiribon*, 33, 35
*tanshoku-dori*, 33
*Teikan Zusetsu*, 14
*Tengu no Dairi*, 148–51
*Tōken Meiran*, 14
Tokiwa, 51, 52, 55, 76–79, 81
Tokugawa Ieyasu, 24
*torinoko-gami*, 13
Tosa school, 14, 20
townsman painters, 19–21

*ukiyo-e*, 13, 17, 33
*ukiyozōshi*, 29
*Uraminosuke*, 187–90
*urushi-e*, 17, 19
Ushiwaka. *See* Yoshitsune, Minamoto no
*Usuyuki Monogatari*, 29, 178–81

Wada no Yoshimori, 68, 104, 106–7
*Wada Sakamori*, 104–7
war tales, *tanrokubon* editions of, 18, 26–27, 41–72
woodblock printing, 11, 14, 17

*Yamato-e*, 13, 15, 20, 21
*Yashima*, 34
*Yokohama-e*, 13
*yokohon. See* Oblong books
Yokoyama Shigeru, 15, 28
Yoritomo, Minamoto no, 51, 60, 67, 86–88, 100, 151, 195, 197
Yoshitomo, Minamoto no, 45, 46, 47, 48, 51, 52, 79, 148, 151
Yoshitsune, Minamoto no, 27, 51, 52–61, 81–82, 92, 95, 96, 99, 122-23, 148, 151, 156, 159
*Yuriwaka Daijin*, 116–20
*Yūzū Nenbutsu Engi*, 12

定価12,000円
in Japan

この画像は、崩し字（くずし字）で書かれた日本の古典籍（変体仮名を含む草書体）のページです。文字が非常に崩れており、正確な翻刻は困難です。